W9-BZQ-639

Let AMERICA Live

STELLA IMMANUEL, MD

CHARISMA
HOUSE

Most Charisma Media products are available at special quantity discounts for bulk purchase for sales promotions, premiums, fundraising, and educational needs. For details, call us at (407) 333-0600 or visit our website at www.charismamedia.com.

Let America Live by Stella Immanuel, MD
Published by Charisma House, an imprint of Charisma Media
600 Rinehart Road, Lake Mary, Florida 32746

This book or parts thereof may not be reproduced in any form, stored in a retrieval system, or transmitted in any form by any means—electronic, mechanical, photocopy, recording, or otherwise—without prior written permission of the publisher, except as provided by United States of America copyright law.

Unless otherwise noted, all Scripture quotations are taken from the King James Version of the Bible.

Scripture quotations marked ASV are from the American Standard Bible.

Scripture quotations marked ESV are from the Holy Bible, English Standard Version. Copyright © 2001 by Crossway Bibles, a division of Good News Publishers. Used by permission.

Scripture quotations marked MEV are from the Modern English Version. Copyright © 2014 by Military Bible Association. Used by permission. All rights reserved.

Scripture quotations marked NIV are taken from the Holy Bible, New International Version®, NIV®. Copyright © 1973, 1978, 1984, 2011 by Biblica, Inc.® Used by permission of Zondervan. All rights reserved worldwide. www.zondervan.com. The "NIV" and "New International Version" are trademarks registered in the United States Patent and Trademark Office by Biblica, Inc.®

Scripture quotations marked NKJV are taken from the New King James Version®. Copyright © 1982 by Thomas Nelson. Used by permission. All rights reserved.

Scripture quotations marked NLT are from the Holy Bible, New Living Translation, copyright © 1996, 2004, 2007. Used by permission of Tyndale House Publishers, Inc., Wheaton, IL 60189. All rights reserved.

Scripture quotations marked NLV are taken from the *New Life Version*, copyright © 1969 and 2003. Used by permission of Barbour Publishing, Inc., Uhrichsville, Ohio 44683. All rights reserved.

Copyright © 2021 by Stella Immanuel, MD
All rights reserved

Visit the author's website at drstellamd.com.

Cataloging-in-Publication Data is on file with the Library of Congress.
International Standard Book Number: 978-1-63641-096-8
E-book ISBN: 978-1-63641-097-5

This book contains the opinions and ideas of its author. It is solely for informational and educational purposes and should not be regarded as a substitute for professional medical treatment. The nature of your body's health condition is complex and unique. Therefore, you should consult a health professional before you begin any new exercise, nutrition, or supplementation program or if you have questions about your health. Neither the author nor the publisher shall be liable or responsible for any loss or damage allegedly arising from any information or suggestion in this book.

While the author has made every effort to provide accurate internet addresses at the time of publication, neither the publisher nor the author assumes any responsibility for errors or for changes that occur after publication. Further, the publisher does not have any control over and does not assume any responsibility for author or third-party websites or their content.

21 22 23 24 25—9 8 7 6 5 4 3 2 1
Printed in the United States of America

CONTENTS

ACKNOWLEDGMENTS

THIS BOOK IS dedicated first to the Holy Spirit, my commander in chief.

To my beautiful girls, Mima and Bernette—I pray the hand of the Holy Spirit stays heavy on you.

To all my spiritual sons and daughters God has given me to mentor, who pray and work with me daily—keep your sword in one hand and work with the other as in the days of Nehemiah. God sees your labor, and you will not go unrewarded. I may be in the forefront, but you are just as deserving of the crown of this battle. May His grace continue to uphold us, in Jesus' name.

To the trench fighters who will not take no for an answer, the Frontline doctors who stood up and continue to stand strong in the face of tremendous persecution—you are today's heroes.

To the staff of Rehoboth Medical Center and Frontline MDs telehealth—you have stood up despite the threat of persecution to take care of the American people. You are appreciated by America. Only eternity will show just how many lives we saved. May the Lord remember us for good.

To all those who proofread, edited, and designed this book, and to those who contributed to it—I pray that they hear us.

To my spiritual parents, Rev. Mosy and Gloria Madugba, who were unwavering anchors in my life way before the Lord promoted me—thank you. Daddy Mosy taught me territorial warfare, and under his mentorship I learned how to occupy the position God placed before me. The Lord was so gracious to me to place them in my house just as things heated up in July of 2020. They were the anchor that kept me steady through the confusion of going global in this battle. Their reassuring presence was indispensable. They answered my ministry phone and sifted through the thousands of messages coming in each day. They screened interviews, answered emails, and prayed with me and for me. Daddy Mosy is what I describe as "calm fire." He would tell me to fight back and not back down. He reminded me that I was God's warrior princess, the Esther of my generation, and that I was trained for this moment.

To my father in the Lord, Dr. D. K. Olukoya, under whose mantle I trained to be a warrior and have found refuge and safety in ministry—thank you.

To those who went before me—Dr. Didier Raoult, Dr. Robin Armstrong, and Dr. Vladimir Zelenko—your voices gave me the courage to jump into the fray and join the battle. You are my heroes!

And lastly, to the unsung heroes who died needlessly in this battle, the hundreds of thousands around the world who died in hospitals alone and away from their families while we debated science—may the Lord comfort those you left behind to mourn the senseless loss. For your sake we will continue to fight. Your blood will not be shed in vain.

May God show humanity mercy and deliver us from our strong enemy, in Jesus' name. May your life be impacted enough as you read to stand up and join the fight. God bless you and God bless the United States of America, in Jesus' name.

—Dr. Stella Immanuel
At His Service
Jesus Is Lord
DRSTELLAMD.COM

PART I

Those from among you shall build the old waste places; you shall raise up the foundations of many generations; and you shall be called the Repairer of the Breach, the Restorer of Streets to Dwell In.

—ISAIAH 58:12, NKJV

Chapter 1

STEPPING ONTO THE NATIONAL STAGE

I STOOD THERE IN the bright sunshine on the steps of the US Supreme Court, head held high and hands clasped confidently in front of me. On either side of me stood other doctors—all of us wearing our white lab coats—from different states, with different specialties, and from a number of different ethnic and religious backgrounds. A few cottony clouds graced the blue, majestic sky as behind us a fountain bubbled, symbolizing life and joy—much of which had been drained from our country in the crazy months following the appearance of a treatable virus called COVID-19 on the world scene.

Like the others with me, I was proud to be in the nation's capital that July day in 2020 because in the midst of a flurry of health-related lies in our nation, a credible, practicing group of physicians was finally going to present the truth. But even we didn't know how far-reaching this press conference would become.

Congressman Ralph Norman of South Carolina bravely introduced our group, which had just concluded a conference dealing with the reality behind COVID-19 and what those of us on the front lines recommended doing about it. Now, as

3

physicians and private individuals, we were going public with our professional opinions, which were backed by results.

Dr. Bob Hamilton of Santa Monica, California, who had practiced medicine for thirty-six years by that time, stepped up first and spoke forcefully and compassionately about how the nation's children were being treated unfairly by teachers' unions, which insisted on nonscientific rules and guidelines to "protect" kids from a virus that posed little harm to them. He exposed the unions' efforts to shut down charter schools—a political agenda as warped and blind as their harmful COVID response. His words were clear and urgent, coming from a man who had devoted his life to helping people get well, only to see our nation's "leaders" propose cures worse than the problem presented by COVID.

Dr. Hamilton wrapped up his brief, powerful message, and then it was my turn. Dr. Gold, our de facto leader, smiled and gestured for me to step up to the mic. I prayed continually as I had prayed throughout the day, and the peace and power of God rushed through me as I calmly began to speak.

"Hello. I am Dr. Stella Immanuel," I said, speaking to the nation for the first time. "I'm a primary care physician in Houston, Texas. You know, I actually went to medical school in West Africa—Nigeria—where I took care of malaria patients, treated them with hydroxychloroquine...so I am actually used to these medications. I am here because I have personally treated over 350 patients with COVID—patients that have diabetes, patients that have high blood pressure, patients that have asthma, old people. I think my oldest patient is ninety-two. Eighty-seven-year-olds. And the result has been the same: I put them on hydroxychloroquine, I put them on zinc, and I put them on [azithromycin]—and they are all well. For the past few months, I have taken care of over 350 patients and have not lost one—not a diabetic, not somebody with high blood pressure, not somebody with asthma, not an old person. We have not lost one patient.

"And on top of that, I have put myself, my staff, and many doctors that I know on hydroxychloroquine for prevention because by the very mechanism of action, it works early as a prophylactic. We see...ten to fifteen COVID patients every day. We give them breathing treatments. We only wear surgical masks. None of us has gotten sick. It works. So right now, I came here to Washington, DC, to say, 'America, nobody needs to die.'"

With each word and sentence I spoke, I felt the Holy Spirit welling up in celebration and support of our message. He is the Spirit of liberty, not of death, lies, and torment such as the American people were experiencing at the hands of so-called medical "experts" and politicians. No! Our God is a God of freedom, which He gave to humanity so we would seek His wisdom and answers in all areas of life—including in the realm of infectious diseases and physical ailments. As I continued to declare the truth over America, I could almost hear the lies snapping off people's minds like broken rubber bands. In that moment, freedom was once again emanating from our nation's capital.

"I'm upset," I continued. "Why I'm upset is that I see people that cannot breathe. I see parents walk in; I see a diabetic sit in my office knowing that this is a death sentence, and they can't breathe. And I hug them and I tell them, 'It's going to be OK. You're going to live.' And we treat them and they live. None has died. So if some fake science, some person sponsored by all these fake pharma companies comes out and says,

'We've done studies and they found out that it doesn't work,' I can tell you categorically, it's fake science. I want to know who is sponsoring that study. I want to know who is behind it, because there is no way I can treat 350 patients and counting and nobody is dead and they all did better."

When you speak the words of God, they flow freely out of you, and they tend to gain momentum, like a river growing wider and faster as it travels to the ocean. I felt this surge inside myself and continued: "I'm a true testimony. So I came here, to Washington, DC, to tell America nobody needs to get sick. I told them about the treatment I had been giving people, consisting of hydroxychloroquine, zinc, and azithromycin. I know you people want to talk about a mask. Hello! You don't need a mask....I know they don't want to open schools. No, you don't need people to be locked down."[1] I knew from my experience there are effective tools for prevention and treatment.

By this point I knew I had stepped boldly into the moment for which God had created me before time began. What I didn't realize was how far and wide that message would spread within just minutes and hours. I was told later that America's Frontline Doctors' press conference was one of the most viral videos in all history. God used it as a hammer blow to the false narrative of politically correct "science," which sought to enslave the American people through fear, misdiagnoses, and crippling guidelines and public health policies.

For me personally, and for all of us who stood there that day, the effect was profoundly transforming as well. Within minutes I went from being an unknown physician in Houston to a national spokeswoman for truth, along with my colleagues. God had prepared me for that moment, and as my life suddenly changed and the enemy fought back hard against our message and our very lives, I felt God's peace and preparation taking me through to victory—just as He had done throughout my life and just as He will do with our nation.

I want to tell you more about how God did what He did that day by preparing my life in advance and positioning me exactly where I needed to be when this virus caused the world to spiral into a kind of chaos. You will learn that I am a Bible-believing Christian, an ordained minister of the gospel, and the founder of Fire Power Ministries church in Katy, Texas. I simultaneously run a private clinic in Houston and am a licensed physician practicing in the state of Texas. Regardless of who may or may not like it, in my life there is no separation of church and state; I practice what I believe, and I believe what I practice. I am a woman of both science and the Spirit. I am grateful that you have picked up this book and given it your attention, as its message is incredibly urgent—so urgent, in fact, that it's actually a matter of life and death, your life and the lives of your loved ones, as well as that of our entire nation and planet. All people alive, and those yet to be born, are unquestionably affected by the information contained in this modest book.

Part of my message has to do with the efficacy of hydroxychloroquine, an antimalarial drug and prophylactic (preventive) that has been safely used for decades to treat everyone from infants to the elderly.[2] In fact, in West Africa, where I grew up, taking the preventive "Sunday-Sunday medicine," as the locals call it, is common. Plenty of my countrymen are familiar with this concoction of readily available drugs in the "quine" family, hydroxychloroquine among them, which is taken to ward off malaria. But even with my history and familiarity with hydroxychloroquine, which has become a rather controversial drug (for reasons I will go into later), I had no idea when I stepped up to the mic that day in DC—and, unwittingly, onto the national stage—that my recommendation of it as a safe and effective treatment for COVID-19 would incite such an immediate and controversial reaction. There was not only controversy surrounding my claims but great contempt for them and for me as well. Even before my moment in the spotlight, in fact, there was an inexplicable resistance, not just in our country but around the world, to hydroxychloroquine as a coronavirus treatment. And while I do have an incredible number of supporters, for which I am most grateful, and I'm certainly not the only vocal proponent of the drug, the public contempt and pushback I've received have come from seemingly everywhere: political leaders and commentators, social media influencers, both real and imagined, so-called experts, internet trolls, and even many of my fellow doctors and medical industry colleagues...many of whom *know* I am speaking the truth!

This explosion of controversy points to the power of that watershed day in July 2020 when we spoke out for truth on the Supreme Court steps. Having the world's spotlight turned on me—along with its accompanying criticism—has changed my life. Yet I wouldn't change a thing. If given the chance, I would do it all over again, even louder than before. That is because lives are tragically at stake, and hydroxychloroquine has the potential to save those lives. It could potentially bring an end to the death toll COVID-19 has exacted on our nation since early 2020. My total belief in the suitability of hydroxychloroquine as a treatment for the coronavirus is the inspiration behind this book and at the heart of its cry to the American government and powers that be: let America live!

To be clear, my advocacy of hydroxychloroquine comes

with strong medical support. What I've said about it and continue to proclaim is based on more than twenty-eight years as a medical practitioner. In other words, it's based on both hands-on experience and success. To date my team and I have treated with hydroxychloroquine more than seven thousand coronavirus-infected or symptomatic patients at my Houston clinic and online via telemedicine, and of that number, only eight precious souls, all of whom were in advanced stages of the disease, passed away. Yes, you read that correctly: out of the seven-thousand-plus virus-affected patients I've treated, 99 percent are alive and well—and their recovery is directly attributable to a prescribed cocktail heavy on hydroxychloroquine. We have also put over twenty thousand patients on prophylaxis, with most never getting the disease despite exposure. A few that did had mild symptoms.

These results beg the question "Why have the US government and the Centers for Disease Control and Prevention made a concerted effort to conceal the truth about hydroxychloroquine, arguably COVID-19's most effective treatment?" Not only have government-sponsored and political organizations been trying to pull the wool over our nation's collective eyes concerning hydroxychloroquine, going so far as to mock, discredit, and even villainize those who, like me, have become vocal advocates of it, but I am now fully convinced that there exists an evil, diabolical conspiracy of widespread cover-up and misinformation to mislead Americans—and people around the world—concerning the truth about COVID-19, including where it came from and how to treat it. For this reason, I felt compelled to carve time out of my intensely busy schedule treating patients six days per week, before ministering to my congregation on Sundays, to "tell the truth and shame the devil," as the saying goes. I feel I must expose to the public what too many of our nation's leaders and experts have refused to reveal. What is their motive in withholding such precious, potentially lifesaving information from the American people? I'll have more on that later, but let me assure you now that this book was written for the singular purpose of making you, the reader, fully aware of what's going on—in the medical industry, in the political arena, and in the spiritual realm—pertaining to COVID-19 and how its emergence has amplified and exposed the intense reality of the end-time narrative in which we are living, perhaps more than any historical event that preceded it.

For all that I share, I invite you to draw your own conclusions. I will unapologetically present my personal opinions and beliefs as an evangelical Christian who lives by the Bible and believes in the power of prophecy and the reality of God-given dreams. I will share some things that undoubtedly will make you think and search your Bible for answers regarding our present reality. I will also share pertinent medical data, all factual and true.

As one chosen to speak to the nation at such a time as this, let me begin by telling you who I am—who God made me to be—and how I came to be one of His standard bearers in the medical community and the church at this moment in history.

Chapter 2

AFRICAN BEGINNINGS

FROM THE TIME of my very first memories at the age of four, I wanted to be a doctor.

Perhaps this desire came from my mother, who always told me she wanted to be a nurse but ended up being a teacher. As a result of that, she decided I was going to be a doctor and achieve a greater height than she. She probably programmed me to want to be a doctor, but all I can say is, the desire to be a doctor has always been in me. I don't remember a day without it.

I grew up in a middle-class family in Bali Nyonga, in the Central African country of Cameroon, where I was born. My parents, both teachers, instilled in all their children a strong desire to be well educated. It amazes me sometimes when people talk about Africa as if people over there live in trees, coming down from them to play with animals. People ask me about safaris, and I shrug and say I never went on one and saw my first elephant in the Bronx Zoo in New York. We grew up in the real Africa, not in the Africa of some people's imaginations.

Our family enjoyed what I consider a regular life. I attended private schools and was more of a tomboy in those days, hanging out with friends and getting into fights as boys would.

Thank God I didn't grow up in a neighborhood full of gangs or drugs, so I was never exposed to drugs. My parents were extremely strict and had no problem spanking me if I messed up. These days many parents allow their children to make decisions about their futures while they are yet young and foolish instead of strongly starting them on the path of success. In my family we did not have a choice; we had to go to school and make something of our lives. My parents would have beaten the living daylights out of us if we had dropped out of school!

I had cousins who lived with us at different times, whom my parents tried to train, but because my parents were strict, most of my cousins did not stay. As for me, I had nowhere to run to. There were times I wished I could trade parents, but today I'm thankful for the tough love and discipline they instilled in me. They did a good job, because all their children are college graduates, with two doctors and a few nurses among us. Children do not usually feel good when disciplined, but when you submit to discipline, it builds the fruit of righteousness. That is the kind of environment I grew up in, and because it so happened that my parents were teachers in the primary school I attended, they wanted to set an example with their own children. I am so thankful today for that push, and I'm thankful my parents are still alive to see their daughter become a strong voice for good in the world. They are proud of what their little girl has become. I also thank God I did not grow up in these times as a tomboy, because I could easily have been told I'm gay or something like that when in fact I was just a tomboy.

When I finished high school, I left for Nigeria. My uncle was a microbiologist at the University of Calabar in southern Nigeria. It was under his guardianship that I secured admission to study medicine at that university.

Medical school was fun. People often view medicine as stressful, but I found it enjoyable. I admit that in my university days in Nigeria, I was a party freak. I was just lucky to have been blessed by God with a brain that enabled me to absorb and retain information easily. I probably would have achieved more as a student if I had been more studious, but I loved to party with friends, who as art students often wondered how a medical student was able to find time to socialize as I did. I would spend three hours or so at a party and still return to the dorm to read and pass my test. Those friends who chose to party with me soon realized, after some failed and had to repeat the year, that it was not a good idea to follow me. Thank God for the brain He gave me!

Back in high school, one of my teachers had said I wasn't going to be successful because instead of reading, I was busy dancing with younger classmates. I was always a lively and passionate person who liked to play. In college I was just as passionate for the world and devil as I am passionate for God now. Somehow, by the grace of God, I graduated from the university. I think God's hand was upon me, because many times I got into trouble or found myself in situations that could easily have led to my death and I was delivered. We did many reckless things. We would leave campus and drive several hours to Port Harcourt to party and drive back tipsy. I remember going to a party and getting drunk and driving back and not getting involved in an accident. I believe the hand of God was upon me, protecting me and others, because some of my friends dropped out of medical school, while others ended up spending two extra years getting their degrees.

As a foreign student in Nigeria, on a Cameroonian scholarship and with parents who also gave me money, I lived a privileged life, and I would help pay the school fees of some others who could not afford it. After graduating from the University of Calabar, my passion was to become a surgeon. My goal at that time was to go to London, train as a surgeon, and then go back home to work. At the time of my graduation, my mind was set on training in England, but because of the declarations I had been making since my early days, I had already programmed my future: I was going to America! As far back as my high school days I used to say I would go to America when I grew up, and those plans prevailed even when I tried to change course. There are times in life when we plan things that seem to be derailed along the way, but they still end up coming to pass.

That is what happened to me. Things did not work out to go to England, and destiny brought me to the United States, where God had much more for me than I could have dared to expect.

Chapter 3

ARRIVING IN AMERICA!

I ARRIVED IN MINNESOTA in July. When I came out of the airport, I stomped my feet on the ground and said, "I have arrived in the land of the free and home of the brave, and I'm going to possess the nation. I will be highly successful and become a millionaire in this country by age thirty-five." Such was my declaration—bold for such a young person coming from a foreign country, but my conviction was strong that it would be true.

By September, Minnesota had turned freezing cold, so I packed my bags and ran down to Houston, where I had family. Then I traveled around a bit and ended up in New York. I immediately set out to take my board exams so I could practice medicine here. I did all kinds of odd jobs to raise money for my study materials and tests. At one point I worked in a homeless shelter as a security guard, living in a one-room apartment in Brooklyn. As a security guard, I mainly sat around and watched over the people in the shelter. I would study for my exams as I worked. People around me doubted my qualifications. "How can she say she's a doctor and be working in a homeless shelter?" some asked. They thought I was a fraud, but God's plan was working in me.

After a while, I got another job as a nursing assistant, but the patient I was assigned to care for did not like me. He preferred a White woman to me. He was mean and would do all manner of nasty things, including defecate on the bed so I had to clean it. He wanted to frustrate me and scare me away, but I did not quit the job. I needed the money to pay my bills, so I stayed put. I also did some phlebotomy work, which, among other things, required me to move around Manhattan drawing blood from people.

After passing the first two parts of the US Medical Licensing Examination (USMLE), I began scouting for a medical residency. It was during that period that I met the man who later became my husband and the father of my children. When I got pregnant, I moved to Houston to be with family, and there I had my baby girl. Months after her birth, in 1995, I decided to move back to New York to try to get into a residency program. I felt it would be easier to get the residency in New York than in Texas. My then "baby daddy" was living in Illinois, acting up, and not being supportive. Things were rough, especially after I failed that July to match into a residency program. I did not have much money, had a baby, and could not get a job. I had to put my baby on welfare, Medicaid, and food stamps to make ends meet. With rent and utilities staring me in the face each month, we barely made it. For eight months we struggled in New York. I used to cry all the time and would turn to my little girl and say, "Ask the angels to give Mommy a job, or we will starve in New York!" I would hold her, rock her, and cry. She was about six months old then. She would look at me as if she knew what I was going through.

I guess my little girl decided to help by running a high fever. I took her to the Bronx-Lebanon ER. On arriving, I saw that one of the ER doctors was African, so I told the staff doctor I wanted to be attended by him. When the African doctor began looking at my little girl, I told him I was a doctor and had passed my exams but had not been able to secure a residency.

"Oh, I'm finishing here in two weeks; my position will be vacant," he told me.

He was a pediatrician, but I didn't think I wanted to be a pediatrician.

"I don't know about pediatrics," I told him. "I want to do family practice."

He smiled and said, "Don't worry. You will love being a pediatrician."

The next day, I brought him my résumé, and he took it to the program director, who was kind and called me the next day. I came in for an interview, and he said, "OK, you can start in two weeks." That is how I went from being on welfare to starting residency and earning more than $40,000 a year. True to what the pediatrician I met that night in the ER had told me, I really enjoyed being a pediatrician.

Marriage Journey

Interestingly, around the time I secured the job, in November 1995, my daughter's father, whom I had not seen for eight months, was visiting Cameroon. We hailed from the same village there, and he called me before traveling to ask whether I had things to send home that he could help me deliver. I said I would think about it but then ignored him.

When he arrived in Cameroon, he went to see my family with his family. His attitude had changed, and he was now acting nice and apologizing to everybody. So they started calling me, saying, "He's such a good guy. You should marry him." I thought, "You guys don't know what he did to me." Still,

I remembered when I first met him at a party. I had told a friend I was with, "You see that dude right there? I'm going to marry him. That's my husband." My friend was like, "What?" But it happened as I predicted. Even though things had gone crazy and we had gone our separate ways, when he traveled to Cameroon and my family and his family members weighed in, we got back together and got married. My own mouth had prophesied it when I first laid eyes on him.

In my second year in residency, I got pregnant again and my second daughter was born. I spent much of that period thinking about how to get a little more sleep because I had a toddler and a newborn baby. It was rough being pregnant, caring for a toddler, and completing my residency while puking for nine months. I still wonder how I survived it. It was God's grace and mercy, and with the support of people such as my adviser, somehow I managed to complete my residency.

My husband and I were about to move to Alexandria, Louisiana, where I had found a job, when our marriage completely broke down. It had been faltering through the last year of residency. He came to help me move and set up the new place in Alexandria, and between that time and when I finished my residency, when he was supposed to conclude his own studies, the marriage dissolved. We went our separate ways until we divorced. He died a few years after remarrying. May the Lord bless his soul.

A NEW HOME

I had been living in Alexandria for more than a decade when I had a strange, disturbing dream.

I was outside and saw people moving around all over the place as if under the control of an unseen force. Strange music, the kind one might hear in a horror movie, played in the background, indicating danger. I could tell that people's minds were being taken over, and they began dancing to this zombie-like music in increasing numbers. I screamed to the pastors in Alexandria, "Come and help me pray—something is taking over the minds of people!" But the pastors were busy doing their programs in their churches: going to weddings, men's breakfasts, youth meetings, and so on. I cried and cried, and still nobody came.

Eventually a lady I believe was an angel came and joined me. We would stop one person and pray, and the person would snap out of it. When the person snapped out of it, he or she would join us in praying for the next person. As we were praying for people and snapping them out of their mind control, I woke up from the dream.

"Lord," I cried, "people's minds are being taken over!" In a way, what I had seen in the dream was not that different from what the world was beginning to look like: the minds of people, especially those of our youths, taken over, programmed with crazy thoughts. But the dream showed this happening at a whole nother level.

The Lord then brought to mind an experience I'd had in August 2004, when I was just starting to move into the realm of spiritual warfare. At that time, the Lord spoke to me, not in a loud voice but clearly in my heart: "Teach My people how to fight. My warriors are wounded and hurting. My army is wounded and hurting. Teach them how to fight. I will send them to you. Do not be afraid; I will send them to you."

That commission and the mind-control dream gave me an even greater burden to pray.

I had moved to Alexandria in 1998 to open a pediatric clinic and had really given my life to the Lord at that time. Within months I noticed that when I prayed for people, they would start rolling on the floor as demons came out of them. When I spoke or sang from the pulpit, people would start experiencing deliverance from demons as well. This also happened later, when I put some of my preaching and programs on YouTube. Some viewers would actually throw up and experience demonic deliverance while watching! This happened also on prayer phone calls I was involved in. Wild stuff was happening, and it all seemed to relate back to deliverance from demons.

On the career side, I wanted to keep my general-medicine skills, so in addition to having a pediatric clinic, I also worked in local emergency rooms. Before that, I worked in the state hospital called Huey P. Long Medical Center. While working in my practice, I also performed emergency medicine in small local hospitals all over Louisiana.

Two years into working in the emergency rooms, my practice started booming. I was the only doctor at that time seeing Medicaid patients in my town. I had decided to take care of the medically underserved, remembering my eight months on Medicaid with my daughter. It was rewarding to watch patients grow from teens to young mothers who brought their own children to me. I became a role model for a lot of the young Black girls and enjoyed counseling them on their careers and other topics. Parents would drag their teens to me to give them a scolding, and I attended a number of graduations, weddings, and so on.

I also threw myself into spiritual warfare and praying for great revival and a move of God in that city and our nation. I had always felt that burden to pray for God to move, and

I discovered that one of the roadblocks in Alexandria was a strong Masonic presence. Many people don't seem to realize how diabolical the Masons are. A lot of the apprentice Masons are just regular people looking to make friends and create political or business relationships to help them succeed, but as they go higher and higher to the second and third degrees, they see that the Masons worship the Great (or Grand) Architect of the Universe. Masons actually recruit in churches. I used to preach about this on the radio in Alexandria, and some Baptist pastors, when they saw me on the road, were terrified. They knew that I knew what they were doing.

By 2011 I was beginning to feel restless in Alexandria and sensed that my destiny belonged somewhere else. My spiritual daughters and I did a hundred-day prayer program in my house. Members of the Fire Power ministry I had founded came from Tennessee, New York, and all over the world during that time, staying for a week, praying, and then returning home. For one hundred days we stayed in the house and on the property and did not come out. We prayed round the clock for the city and nation, and God began to show us a whole lot of things about the United States.

At the height of our prayer time, on day ninety-nine of the program, I woke up and was getting ready to go to my shift at the prayer room when right at my door I saw a snake. My room is in the far back of the house. How a snake came in through the front door, slithered all the way over cement, and got to my bedroom door was not even comprehensible! I screamed and called someone to help me. We killed the snake, took it outside, and burned it.

That night, I had a dream. In it I saw a lot of men had come onto my property. When you are spiritually full and have been praying for a hundred days, you are like a giant in the Spirit, so I started beating these men up, picking them up by their heads, using one to slap the other, and carrying one of them like a club and using him to knock the other ones around. I knocked them against a tree, beat them, slapped them, jammed their heads together, picked them up, and threw them. This lasted for fifteen or twenty minutes in the dream, until finally one of them said, "OK, stop, stop, stop."

What he said next puzzled me greatly.

"You cannot kill us," he said. "We are genetically modified human beings. We are a different kind of people. There are a lot of us around. It's just not our time yet. When our time comes, we're going to manifest. We come in peace. We just wanted to check out what you people were doing here."

Then they told me the name of someone I knew in real life who is one of them. They said, "If she could just stop trying to run away, her life would be better." This explained so much about this girl. In the real world I had thought the girl was bipolar, as she would sometimes hit the floor and scream in church. I now realized why she acted that way. Their recommendation to her was to surrender to who she was so her life would be better.

I woke up and immediately went to the Bible, praying, "Father, whatever You show me in the dream has to have something in the Bible that backs it up." I started reading Scripture and searching, and the burden I'd always had for the nation increased even more. I started driving around the city every day, praying in the Holy Ghost for two hours at a time. I prayed over every place I saw, and one day while I was doing that, I had the thought, "Alexandria doesn't feel like where I'm supposed to be." I knew God had called me to America to be a prophet of God to the nations, though at that time, I was just a small hometown preacher. Now I became convinced that His call for me would not manifest in Alexandria but somewhere else.

My assistant and I decided to pray earnestly for God to show us where I was supposed to be. We prayed all night, from 11:00 p.m. to 5:00 a.m. We said, "Father, show me my location. Just like the prophet Elijah, whom You told to go to the brook Cherith and You would have ravens there to feed him. Lord, show me where I'm supposed to be, my exact location, where it is ordained for me to be. Show me where You have kept ravens to feed me. Show me the place where I'm supposed to fulfill my destiny." We prayed that one thing all night long.

When I went to sleep, I had a dream that I was in Houston doing a program right where my clinic is now. People were all over the place. When I woke up, I said, "Whoa! God wants me to move to Houston." To be candid, Houston was not my first choice—it wasn't even on my list! I did not want to move there because I have a lot of family members in Houston who are nosy, and I did not want them prying into my everyday life. I would have preferred to go to Dallas or Atlanta or to stay in Alexandria, where I was comfortable and where one of my children was in college and the other was about to finish high school. But I knew the dream was from the Lord, so I said, "We're going to Houston to do programs."

Though I couldn't fully see it yet, Houston would become the place of my inheritance and the platform for my influence.

Chapter 4

BACK TO DELIVERANCE

THE NEXT MONTH, my team and I went to Houston and put together a citywide prayer program at a cost of $10,000 to $15,000. We advertised the event in the *Houston Chronicle* and fasted for three days with no food or water. We rented a nice hall and chairs in a hotel, but that evening, only five or so people came for the program. I was so discouraged afterward. I said, "Lord, You told me to come here. I came, I did what You asked me to do, and just those people came? Well, I'm just gonna pack my bags and go back to Louisiana and continue with my business." That night, I practically cried myself to sleep—and the Lord gave me a very strange but meaningful dream.

In it I was in Alexandria. Somebody told me to take care of two children, one about two years of age, the other about four years of age. But I replied, "I'm not taking care of those children! I'm not dealing with it, no, no, no!"

As I started walking away, a car passed by and hit the children, and they fell down. When I saw what had happened, I screamed and said, "They told me to take care of those children, and I refused, and now a car has hit them." I thought they were dead, so I ran over to them, and by God's grace, they were not dead. I was crying and apologizing profusely for refusing to take care of them in the first place. They stood up, and I saw that the two-year-old had a bruise on his right leg, so I bent down and put my hand on the right leg to pray for the injury. I must have prayed for five minutes, and when I said, "Amen," and opened my eyes, the two-year-old was now six years old! He said, "Mum, you've been praying for four years. We are in 2016, and the world has changed."

I said, "What?"

"The world has changed," he said again. He meant it in such a way to indicate that evil had taken over the world.

I got up and started walking around to see what this world was like. Yes, indeed, it had changed. Demons were walking around with humans in groups of two or three, like friends would. Mermaids were swimming in pools with people. Because I was in the spirit, I could see who was a human being and who was not, but I don't know whether the people themselves realized that the other "people" were demons. Mermaids jostled people in the water and swam around like it was normal. Other demons walked around, talking with humans who did not realize they were demons. "They've taken over the world," I said as I walked around, documenting what I saw.

I entered a mall. Everything they were selling was demonic. I greeted a young man, a Christian, but he appeared to be so fatigued. I asked him, "What is going on?" He said, "Oh, I'm one of you, but I'm kind of tired and drained." So I started going through the mall and documenting what was going on. I entered the mall from what seemed to be the second floor. As I was standing on the balcony, looking down on the inside part of the mall, a force pushed me from behind and I started falling. As I was falling, I screamed and said, "Host of heaven, where are you?" Then a carpet emerged under me, caught me, and put me down. I continued recording what I saw and eventually left.

I woke up, and the dream shook me to the core. Then the Holy Spirit said, "This is why you need to pray, and this is why I needed you to move to Houston."

"OK, I will," I agreed.

From that day forward the intensity of my prayer and hunger for a move of God increased. I preached about it and encouraged my church to pray. I even wrote a book in 2015 called *Ten Point Plan to Disciple America Back to God, portions of which are included in part 3 of this book.*

BACK AND FORTH BETWEEN HOUSTON AND LOUISIANA

The urgency to move quickly to Houston intensified. The place I had seen in a dream was close to my cousin's store, so I told her about it, and she said, "That means you are supposed to be somewhere around me." So we bought a certain property, which had room for the church and a home, and we began praying over it intensively and building it out. All the while, I drove back and forth between Houston and Louisiana to keep my practice running.

I spent all of 2014 going back and forth between Houston and Louisiana, trying to build the church and a house and work at my practice. It was overwhelming in every way. I cried every day and prayed and fasted, doing all kinds of fasts to try to get victory. One of my spiritual daughters had come to join me in the ministry as well, and she felt the effects of this devastating season as well.

I had become so interested in revival that I was focusing much less on my call as a deliverance minister. I really just wanted to pray for revival and for the nation. We finished the church area of the building in the first week of November 2014—and three weeks later I lost my practice. The doctor that was working for me decided to suddenly open her own practice down the street, and with her went most of my patients. She gave me one day's notice.

By now I had used all the money I had and racked up a huge credit card debt, maxing out all my credit cards and using up my savings, to build the church and bookstore. I did it knowing my practice could bring in sufficient money, but now—*boom*! Everything was lost. I went from making $60,000 to $70,000 a month to having $60,000 to $70,000 in monthly bills with no money coming in and a huge credit card bill. My retirement was gone, and so was everything I had.

I cried out, "Lord, what's going on in my life?"

I received no clear direction, and for one year I didn't know what to do. I planned to put the church building back on the market, sell it, and go back to Louisiana and find a job. By April 2015 the taxes amounted to almost $17,000, and I had no money to pay them. Desperate to stop bleeding cash, I decided to put the building under the name of the church so I could be tax-exempt, since the building was in my name. This took a long time but finally became official on April 1, 2015.

The building had flood insurance, but I did not transfer the insurance from my name to the ministry's. Two weeks later, on April 15, the church got flooded. The damage cost about $160,000, and I still did not have a dime. The insurance company refused to pay it because I didn't have any insurable interest; the building was not in my name.

FIGHTING FOR BREAKTHROUGH

I lived upstairs, and we ripped out the whole flooded downstairs. The house stayed in that condition for almost a year. I had no money to fix it. Thank God the church part of the building was not badly damaged, so we continued to have church. But the rest of the house was physically open for almost a year, and we had to walk through the damaged part to go upstairs. That is how I lived for almost a year and a half. It was horrible. I could not even sell the place because the walls were open.

Trying to gain the victory over these massive problems, I kept praying and fasting, driving back and forth weekly between Houston and Louisiana. None of my prayers seemed to budge heaven. Finally, I said, "This is not the devil. I know how to fight the devil. There is something more to this." So I changed what I was doing and went through four days of dry fasting. I called it the "Lazarus fast," or the "resurrection fast," because Lazarus was resurrected after four days. I declared, "This fast is for the resurrection power of the Lord Jesus to enter my life." I would drive all around Louisiana for a couple of hours, then enter Texas and take Clay Road and drive all the way around for another two or three hours. I did that daily.

On the third day of the fast, I was at my clinic in Oakdale, Louisiana. I walked in to grab something before I started driving, and as I was about to enter my room, I spotted a tiny live snake right in front of the door. I got so angry I stamped on it, saying, "Devil, you're under my feet." With my foot I crushed it, and in that moment, I decided to continue the fast to the fourth day. I also had heard from my spiritual parents, Rev. Mosy Madugba and his wife, Gloria, who had people praying for me back home in Nigeria. A message from there said that the witchcraft in Houston had oppressed me and that's what the fight was all about. So I intensified my prayers.

I turned left onto Clay Road that night, and when the clock turned midnight, marking exactly four days on the fast, I ate some cookies and drank some water and continued with my prayers.

"Father, let the resurrection power, the same power that raised the Lord Jesus from the dead, resurrect my life," I pleaded. "I don't know what's going on. Let the resurrection power of the Lord Jesus visit me and visit my whole life."

As I was praying, the Lord spoke to me. His message was so clear in my spirit. He said: "I anointed you. I gave you the kind of anointing most people don't have, and you refused to take care of My people."

In my heart I thought, "What did I do wrong?"

"Yes, you refused to take care of My people," He continued. "You left your calling."

When the Lord speaks, it brings clarity and allows you to see reality. He was right; I had set aside my calling to be a deliverance minister in favor of praying for revival and the nation. This was a serious matter.

"Oh, God, I'm so sorry," I said. "I have taken Your power and grace upon my life for granted. Lord, I am so sorry. Father, if You give me just one more chance, I will do right. Don't take Your anointing off my life. Don't take Your calling away from me. If You just give me one more chance, Lord, I will do right."

Crying, I called one of my spiritual daughters, who has a church in Florida, and said, "Please, Pastor, help me pray. I have sinned."

"What did you do, Mum?" she asked.

I told her I had set aside my calling and the Lord had corrected me for it.

"Yes, when I needed deliverance, I brought my whole church to you," she reminded me.

In fact, she wrote a book saying that breakthrough in her life and ministry came when she visited our ministry with her whole leadership team for deliverance.

"What would have happened to me if at that time I came, you did not want to do deliverance?" she asked me now.

I said, "Please, just beg God for me. I promised the Lord I will do right."

As we prayed together, I felt the glorious release that comes through repentance and return to one's God-given calling. The next day was Sunday, and I announced to the church, "We are a frontline deliverance ministry." Then I told them what had happened and repented before them. Yes, praying for revival is a good thing, but that was not the mandate for my life. God had told me that the revival of this generation is going to be a revival of great deliverance. Revival was going to come through deliverance.

Undoubtedly some people reading this book are ministers of God who have been derailed in their callings, and the heavens over them have closed up. I know the feeling. While I was away from my calling, my heavens were closed. It didn't matter what I tried to do. For two years, as a doctor, I couldn't find a job. I couldn't get a clinic started. I stressed myself out driving back and forth. It was like everywhere I turned, heaven was closed. I even remember calling one of my colleagues one day because I needed $2,500 to pay my staff and I didn't have it. That's how bad it was. I remember the day the light was cut off in the church because I didn't have $700 to pay the light bill.

Sometimes as Christians, when things are not working out, we should stop blaming God and go back to find out where we have sinned. Where have we disobeyed God? Where have we walked away from God's purpose for our lives?

GETTING TO YOUR RIGHT PLACE

This is important because a fish cannot prosper in a tree. A fish has to be in water to prosper. A bird cannot prosper in a river; it has to be flying to prosper. If you are out of position or location, you are not going to prosper. If God told Elijah, "Go to the brook Cherith. I will send ravens to feed you," and Elijah went instead to the Jordan River, he would have starved because the ravens were going to the brook Cherith.

Some of us think that because we have worked for God, it's OK to be rebellious. I thought, "How could I come to Houston, buy a place, spend all my money to build a house for God, and lose everything?" The fact that you are working for God does not allow you to become rebellious. I was rebellious at that time, doing my own thing instead of what God called and anointed me to do.

So we immediately changed and started doing deliverance every week. People started coming as they used to do. A month later I got a job in a pediatric clinic in Louisiana. Upon working again, first on my agenda was to fix the house of God. Then somebody I had worked with years earlier in an emergency room called and said, "Dr. Immanuel, you used to work in emergency rooms. Are you still interested?"

When I had worked in emergency rooms, the pay was about $60 an hour. I asked how much they were paying now. His answer: $120 to $140 an hour. I said, "What! I haven't worked in an ER for a long time."

He said, "No problem. You just have to dust off your skills."

So I did an emergency-medicine boot camp, which took me about a month to finish. I did advanced trauma life support (ATLS), advanced cardiac life support (ACLS), pediatric advanced life support (PALS), and basic life support (BLS) training. I attended an American College of Emergency Physicians conference, which is a four-day training conference for emergency medicine. I did all these in about four months, plus a few shadowing shifts.

On Memorial Day weekend of 2017 I did my first shift in an emergency room again. Nobody wanted to cover that shift because it was a holiday weekend. I got there Friday morning at 8:00 a.m. and left Monday morning at 8:00 a.m. That's a seventy-two-hour shift, and they were paying me something like $110 per hour. I was so thankful to God. I took the money and started fixing the church. Before long I got one or two other shifts in low-volume emergency rooms as well. By June and July I was working around a hundred hours a week, going from one ER to the next, then coming back Saturday for church. I would drive to Louisiana because I didn't have a Texas license. At that time, doctors were required to go to school for another six months, or if they had been out of school for ten years, they could not get a Texas license at all. It was certainly a lot of driving, but in one particular month I made in the neighborhood of $30,000 or $40,000 by working nearly every hour I could.

I took the money and continued fixing the church. Fixing the church was just about the only thing on my mind. I also contributed to a church building project in Nigeria through my spiritual parents. They had just finished a conference and needed to pay the bills, so I helped there too. I believe that if you give, you will reap, so I've always been a giver. I love to be a conduit of God's money. God knows that if He tells me His children need money, I will take care of it. For example, our church frequently houses people for free when they need it, sometimes for a week or more. I also support orphans back home in Africa. I think God has blessed me financially because the spirit of giving has been part of my ministry. My friends always called me "gold fingers" because everything I touched prospered. That was another reason it was so strange to struggle financially for those two years when I was away from my calling.

I finished repairing the church in the first week of August 2017, and during the last week of August, Hurricane Harvey passed through town, and the whole church flooded with up to three feet of water. Harvey devastated many parts of Houston, and I was somewhat traumatized because I was upstairs when the flooding started. The fire department came and rescued us at midnight, having waded through water to get to us. For months I had nightmares of being drowned and things like that. But our insurance was sound this time, and we got paid a whole lot of money, which we used to repair the whole place even better than it was before we bought it! I used the money I made working to set up a bookstore right next to where my clinic is now located. I have always sold Christian books, my books and books of other powerful ministers of the gospel both in America and abroad, to edify believers.

After Hurricane Harvey, I was talking to a lady about possibly getting a medical license in one or two other states, including Kentucky, where I had heard there was a good amount of work. She went online to research it and saw that I could get a Texas license. I told her I couldn't because of the ten-year rule. She said, "No, it's not so anymore."

She was right. I went online and learned that Texas had removed this rule because it needed more doctors. That was how I started applying for my Texas license, which took nine months to obtain. For four years I had driven back and forth from my place of destiny—Houston—to the place of my paycheck—Louisiana. I was so tired, but now those days were over. I purchased the walk-in clinic of a doctor who had owned it for twenty-five years and had built a huge clientele, with cash pay only.

I would soon realize that everything—the extensive driving and praying, the ER work, the loss of my clinic and the acquisition of this new clinic, and so much more—had happened exactly according to God's plan, because within months COVID-19 would hit. If I hadn't lost my practice, I would not have gone back to working in the ER and acquired the skills to treat critically ill patients or comfortably run a walk-in clinic, seeing adults in urgent-care situations. By 2019 I had more than five thousand hours of ER work because I was basically working all week. By now I was adequately trained to be able to take over a general clinic.

If the woman in Louisiana had not taken my clinic and my patients, I would not have started seeing adults. If I had not lost my clinic and had just moved to Houston, I probably would have opened a pediatric clinic and left it at that. I would not have been prepared for the big assignment God had for me. The things done wrong to me were all part of the preparation to be where I was at the time COVID-19 came, to be a voice not only in this nation but worldwide. This was my destiny.

I renamed the clinic Rehoboth Medical Center, from the

verse that says, "The LORD has made room for us, and we will be fruitful in the land" (Gen. 26:22, MEV). Sometimes my mind went back to a dream I'd had in January 2016 in response to my asking God, "This is 2016. What is going to happen?" Here is what I posted about the dream on Facebook on January 12, 2016:

> Recently after I gave the prophetic word for 2016 I have been asking the Lord what exactly was going to happen. Last night the Lord showed me in a vision of the night that there was a major disaster in the Land of America. There had been some kind of attack or something that released a thick whitish gray smoke all over the land. People were covered and it was so thick like a fog. You could not see people in it. But it was causing burning in the eyes and choking but it did not kill them at least not immediately. Just a lot [of] respiratory symptoms. We were in the middle place while on both sides the fog was thick. We were temporarily safe but we knew...it will eventually get to us. Saints it's time for us to get our lives right with God and be rapture ready. I am not saying the rapture is eminent even though I have had several visions of the rapture in recent times. But Saint I feel strongly that something really crazy is about to take place. The safest place will be in God's will. In total obedience. Get [your] life right. Get the gray areas and the little compromises out of your life. Go to the Lord and ask Him to examine your life and bring you in right standing. Get rid of the pride, unforgiveness, little sins. Pray and read the word like crazy. Pray that God will preserve your soul and keep you [rapture ready]. Read the prophetic word and the cautions we need to take to survive this year.
>
> May the angels of the Lord encamp around you and your family to deliver you in Jesus name.[1]

Then I gave this word:

January 13, 2016:

Last night I was asking the Lord for details and what must be done. I found myself at a prayer meeting and people, a lot of people were on the floor crying out and praying for mercy. When I woke up the story of Jonah and Nineveh came so strongly in my spirit. I believe there is still room for God's hand of judgement to be stayed if only we can repent. Not the cute repenting we pretend to do in our prayer meetings but a heart cry to the Lord for mercy. For our wicked ways. I saw so many people but I just don't know how to reach [those] people and call for repentance. [I'm] praying that God will help me. We are all so busy and so caught up in our lives that it's hard to make time for God. This weekend we have a program called three days with God to pull down our mountains. Praying 7 hours a day for three days. Day two is baptism of fire and we will cry out. It's in Houston, Texas. We will try to stream it on Periscope. But join us if you can.

God told Jonah to preach to Nineveh and they repented, and God heard them. They repented with sackcloth and ashes.

Jonah 3: "And the word of the LORD came unto Jonah the second time, saying, Arise, go unto Nineveh, that great city, and preach unto it the preaching that I bid thee. So Jonah arose, and went unto Nineveh, according to the word of the LORD. Now Nineveh was an exceeding great city of three days' journey. And Jonah began to enter into the city a day's journey, and he cried, and said, Yet forty days, and Nineveh shall be overthrown.

"So the people of Nineveh believed God, and proclaimed a fast, and put on sackcloth, from the greatest of them even to the least of them. For word came unto the king of Nineveh, and he arose from his throne, and he laid his robe from him, and covered him with sackcloth, and sat in ashes. And he caused it to be proclaimed and published through Nineveh

by the decree of the king and his nobles, saying, Let neither man nor beast, herd nor flock, taste any thing: let them
not feed, nor drink water: But let man and beast be covered
with sackcloth, and cry mightily unto God: yea, let them
turn every one from his evil way, and from the violence that
is in their hands. Who can tell if God will turn and repent,
and turn away from his fierce anger, that we perish not?

"And God saw their works, that they turned from their
evil way; and God repented of the evil, that he had said that
he would do unto them; and he did it not."

The word of the Lord is coming to you America. REPENT!
REPENT! REPENT![2]

I do believe that the globalists were ready for Hillary
Clinton to take over and bring their one-world, diabolical plan
to finish what Obama had started, but the church had been
praying fervently and God thwarted their plans by allowing
Donald J. Trump to win. Still, my heart was heavy as I realized the people were not hearing the warnings of judgment
from God's prophets such as Apostle John Mulinde and Rabbi
Jonathan Cahn.

The world was about to see an eruption of pseudoscience
used by demonic, power-hungry people to cage, corrupt, and
destroy humanity. The Bible passages about evil seed in the
land—a theme that also appeared in my dramatic spiritual
dream—would seem to manifest and cause chaos in our once
peaceful, stable country. I was about to witness this battle and
take part in it.

Chapter 5

CHINA VIRUS

I WAS SPENDING MOST of my work hours at Rehoboth Medical Center when COVID-19 hit in early 2020. Considering that 15 to 20 percent of our clinic patients are from the Middle East, China, or Japan, we were very concerned about what might happen in the community we served, especially given the alarming reports coming out of China about the virus' danger.

In March 2020, before people had started dying in any great numbers, I went to the Lord to find out what was going on. He gave me a dream. In it I saw light rays like missiles being released from the heavenlies, hitting people on the earth and killing them. As I stood watching, a contraption from the heavens crashed and killed many people. The dream alerted me to what was ahead, and I preached a message calling everyone to pray. To be honest, most who heard the message did not take me seriously, but for my part, I knew that COVID-19 was a very real demonic attack on humanity. My colleagues and church members mostly thought I was being overly intense at that time.

Because I knew it would be serious, my clinic purchased all the personal protection equipment we thought we would need: Tyvek suits, N95 masks, surgical masks, face shields, booties to go over our shoes, and other things. If you look at videos and photographs of our staff during that period, it looks as if we are preparing to go to outer space. I was glad for our preparation because when N95 masks came into short supply later, we mailed some to terrified doctors nationwide.

So my clinic stayed open as the purported two-week lockdown began with the goal of "flattening the curve." I well remember how in mid-March a young lady came to the clinic with flu-like symptoms and ended up in the hospital a few days later, intubated. We saw that this was a serious disease, and my dream underlined its destructive potential.

Interestingly the federal government's approach initially was not to prevent all deaths or the ultimate number of deaths but to keep the medical system from being overwhelmed. Hospitals prepared themselves with equipment and manpower. Nonessential surgeries were postponed and normal appointments put off until the crisis had passed. Then the nation held its breath to see what COVID-19 was really going to be like. In places such as New York, it seemed as if the worst-case scenario was taking place. The media showed dead bodies being carried out by medical personnel in full gear and loaded into freezer trucks in the streets.[1] The numbers seemed staggering as we listened to the reports. Gov. Andrew Cuomo quarantined healthy people and sent sick patients back into nursing homes, needlessly killing thousands because of bad policy, as we later learned.[2]

Then medical professionals began to notice that hospitals were not being overwhelmed after all. Rather, they stood mostly empty, waiting for the surge, which never came. Some teetered on the edge of bankruptcy as profitable surgeries and procedures were indefinitely postponed and COVID patients never arrived in the numbers predicted. Of course, the images from China with people being dragged screaming into quarantine and a dead body on the street were still fresh and raw.[3] Americans mostly agreed to do their part to flatten the curve, but opinions began to diverge about how serious of an outbreak this was and how it should be handled medically.

Mixed signals came from various directions. Doctors began sending distress calls about people being intubated and dying.[4] Nurses and whistleblowers sent out reports about doctors intubating patients wrongly, neglecting patients, even declaring them dead before they were dead.[5] Reports surfaced about doctors being coerced to add COVID to every death certificate,[6] perhaps so medical providers would receive more money from various governments that had set aside billions for COVID relief. It wasn't long before statistics showed people no longer dying in usual numbers from heart disease, cancer, overdoses, or the flu. Rather, everyone was suddenly dying from COVID.[7]

How I Began Using Hydroxychloroquine to Defeat COVID-19

One day early on, a friend of mine who is a pharmacist called to tell me they were using hydroxychloroquine in the treatment of COVID-19. There was information coming out of China, Europe, and other locations that this treatment was very effective.[8] That was exciting news to me because I went to school in West Africa, where we were accustomed to using all these different quinolines. We use hydroxychloroquine, mefloquine, nivaquine, and others in that family of medicines. I did a little bit of research and found an article published in *Virology Journal* in 2005 that said chloroquine was a potent inhibitor of SARS-CoV-1.[9] This was great news, and I immediately started using hydroxychloroquine for COVID patients coming into my clinic. Initially I basically used the malaria dosage. The results were amazing! When we treated a patient who came in within three days of contracting the disease, the person became better quickly. One husband and wife, both in their fifties, arrived for treatment. He had been sick for over a week, and his wife even longer than that. We put them on the same regime. The wife became better within forty-eight hours. The husband took about two weeks to get completely well.

I then saw information from the renowned French micro-biologist Didier Raoult and the doses he was using, and Dr. Vladimir Zelenko and the doses he was using,[10] so I adjusted my regimen accordingly. Initially we used mefloquine until hydroxychloroquine became more readily available, and it worked too with great results.

Since according to the 2005 NIH publication, hydroxychloroquine could be used for prophylaxis (prevention treatment) in addition to stopping advancement and replication of coronavirus (SARS-CoV), it made sense to put my whole staff on bimonthly doses.[11] Some took mefloquine, and others hydroxychloroquine, but we all eventually settled on weekly hydroxychloroquine as the crisis progressed. Thanks to that decision, I never got sick, despite constant exposure to COVID-19.

Doctors Versus Doctors

With all the amazing results we saw with our patients in the clinic, I was excited to share our findings with colleagues on Facebook and in doctor groups I belonged to elsewhere. I told my fellow doctors we were getting tremendous results using hydroxychloroquine with a combination of azithromycin, zinc, and vitamin C. We later added vitamin D. I expected celebration and follow-up questions about our protocols. To my dismay

I was attacked instead! Most of the doctors said it did not work and that we needed a double-blind controlled study. Dr. Anthony Fauci of the Centers for Disease Control and Prevention (CDC), to my greatest surprise, then announced that hydroxychloroquine did not work,[12] though it had been in use for more than sixty-five years with a well-known safety profile.[13]

The US Food and Drug Administration (FDA) had long approved of it, but all of a sudden, doctors were being cautioned about it.[14] For years nobody had bothered much about the QT prolongation (heart issues) it could cause. There are dozens of drugs that have the same QT prolongation.[15] Nobody ever says, "You should check your EKG because these drugs cause QT prolongation" when you take Bactrim[16] or Zithromax[17] or Cipro.[18] There is a list of these drugs that cause QT prolongation, including many drugs in widespread use every day. But all of a sudden, doctors were saying, "Hydroxychloroquine can kill you." I told them, "It's dispensed over the counter in Africa, in India, and many places. No, it doesn't stop your heart. It is safer than Tylenol,"[19] but this mostly fell on deaf ears. I assured people that you can give hydroxychloroquine to babies, the elderly, nursing mothers, pregnant women, and so on. Hydroxychloroquine cannot possibly be that dangerous. Patients with lupus or arthritis take it twice a day for years, with no monitoring or caution.[20] Maybe five years down the line, they are asked to undergo an eye test. Now, all of a sudden, doctors didn't want people to take a five-day course of hydroxychloroquine because it would kill them? That did not make any sense.

My frustration grew when I saw Sanjay Gupta on CNN say that hydroxychloroquine could kill.[21] Gupta is a neurosurgeon who likely has never treated a COVID patient. In our hyperspecialized medical culture, he probably would have no reason to. In parts of Africa and some other parts of the world, doctors train as general practitioners first. In America, people come out of medical school and go into some kind of specialty. So in this country, many doctors lose their general practicing skills because they never trained in the field in the first place. Many of the doctors who vilified hydroxychloroquine were not even clinicians seeing patients! For my part, I grew up taking these medications for malaria weekly for prevention. Now I was caring for patients with these same drugs, and they got better. How could people rush to say they didn't work?

When President Trump said something about hydroxychloroquine, the Democrats lost their collective mind. That launched a full-blown public assault on the drug. Fauci, in that strange voice of his, said all of the pro-hydroxychloroquine info was "anecdotal."[22] (It didn't escape the notice of a friend of mine who looked up the meaning of Fauci in Italian and found it means sickle, like the sickle the angel of death is depicted as carrying in drawings.[23])

Many stories poured forth of people who had been successfully treated with hydroxychloroquine, but the media and the medical community seemed in lockstep with Fauci in making sure people were not treated. A Michigan lawmaker who said her life was saved with hydroxychloroquine was attacked and censured.[24] It was as if something had taken over the brains of these otherwise sensible doctors. All they could repeat was, "Double-blind study, double-blind study." It was beyond puzzling to me and many others.

FAKE SCIENCE

Then came the fake science claiming hydroxychloroquine did not work. A retrospective analysis study was done of very sick patients in the Veterans Affairs (VA) who were given hydroxy-chloroquine, and some of them died anyway.[25] When the study was released, even the VA secretary said that "the records review reported outcomes where hydroxychloroquine alone was provided to our sickest COVID-19 patients. The Veterans who received hydroxychloroquine were at highest risk prior to receiving the medication."[26] Yet CNN's Gupta and other high-profile voices cited this study to claim hydroxychloroquine can kill you and affect the rhythm of your heart.[27] They scared the nation to pieces about hydroxychloroquine, but it was a fraud, a lie. The VA director himself said hydroxychloroquine had been working on middle-aged and younger veterans.[28]

Then a *Lancet* registry analysis study of over ninety-six thousand patients worldwide found that hydroxychloroquine didn't work and was associated with an increased risk of in-hospital mortality and arrhythmia.[29] Because of that the World Health Organization stopped clinical trials of the medication.[30] CNN also announced with all the authority it could muster that hydroxychloroquine doesn't work.[31] The madness was spreading.

Some doctors looked at the *Lancet* study and said, "This is not possible; you cannot, in four months, get the data of almost one hundred thousand people from across so many countries. Show us the data, and let us evaluate it." It turned out their concerns were correct. The data, which was never provided for peer review, "included impossibly high numbers of cases—exceeding official case or death counts for some continents and coming implausibly close for others. Similar data discrepancies were also identified in two previous studies that had relied on the...database."[32] The *Lancet* later withdrew the article, but when it did, CNN did not report it with nearly the same level of attention. They had trumpeted the false findings but did not make noise about the fact that that article was fraudulent and had been withdrawn. Though CNN did not report the retraction, Euronews, according to a report by Alex Ledsom for *Forbes*, reported that "the study was not a clinical trial—it was based on observational analysis run between December 20, 2019 and April 14, 2020."[33]

The retraction in the *Lancet* from three of the authors stated, "After publication of our *Lancet* Article, several concerns were raised with respect to the veracity of the data and analyses conducted by Surgisphere Corporation and its founder and our co-author, Sapan Desai, in our publication."[34]

Another report, by WebMD, stated that "the online medical journal *The Lancet* has apologized to readers after retracting a study that said the anti-malarial drug hydroxychloroquine did not help to curb COVID-19 and might cause death in patients."[35]

The *Lancet* retraction stated, "Our independent peer reviewers informed us that Surgisphere [the company that provided the data] would not transfer the full dataset, client contracts, and the full ISO audit report to their servers for analysis as such transfer would violate client agreements and confidentiality requirements. As such, our reviewers were not able to conduct an independent and private peer review and therefore notified us of their withdrawal from the peer-review process....Based on this development, we can no longer vouch for the veracity of the primary data sources. Due to this unfortunate development, the authors request that the paper be retracted."[36]

The *Lancet* retraction even forced the journal to review its policy regarding papers submitted to it for publication. In the October 10, 2020, issue, it states:

The publication and subsequent retraction in June, 2020, of the Article Hydroxychloroquine or chloroquine with or without a macrolide for treatment of COVID-19: a multinational registry analysis, based on an alleged dataset associated with Surgisphere, prompted us to examine *The Lancet's* peer-review processes to identify ways of further reducing risks of research and publication misconduct. As a result of this review, with immediate effect, we have made changes to the declarations we seek from authors, the data sharing statements we require for published research papers, and the peer-review process for similar papers based on large datasets or real-world data. Changes to the signed declarations by authors in the author statements form will require that more than one author has directly accessed and verified the data reported in the manuscript. We will require that the authors who have accessed and verified underlying data are named in the contributors' statement. For research Articles that are the result of an academic and commercial partnership, one of the authors named as having accessed and verified data must be from the academic team. In addition, all authors will be asked to sign the author statements form to confirm they had full access to the data reported in their Article, and accept responsibility for submitting the Article for publication.[37]

But by this time, the damage to hydroxychloroquine's reputation had been done. Few people read retractions, and few news organizations give them the same attention they gave to the initial, false reports.

Another study, from the University of Minnesota, sought to prove whether hydroxychloroquine can work after exposure, but the results were skewed because some people in the study received hydroxychloroquine a full four days after being exposed. You have to wonder, Was there any bias due to the fact that the Bill and Melinda Gates Foundation gave the University of Minnesota over three million dollars in April

2020 "to provide effective, accessible, scalable treatment for COVID-19"?[38]

Meanwhile, other studies supporting the use of hydroxychloroquine came from France[39] and Yale's Dr. Risch[40] and many other doctors, but these weren't well publicized. When people reported positive news about hydroxychloroquine, they were more likely to be attacked than championed,[41] while doctors like me who were treating patients with it were smeared and lied about.

This noncontroversial drug was suddenly targeted by governments. Interestingly, in late 2019 France began requiring a prescription for hydroxychloroquine, which went into effect in January 2020. Before then hydroxychloroquine was available over the counter there. In Australia hydroxychloroquine was made to look dangerous.[42] The same thing happened in Trinidad and Tobago.[43] A lady from there called me and said hydroxychloroquine had become very difficult to come by in her country. Governments were interfering in the use of the drug at a time of a pandemic, when experienced doctors were telling people that hydroxychloroquine works. That had never happened in history, and it made no sense. They were essentially blocking people from choosing their treatment, and allowing them to die.

As I sounded the alarm about these things in the first couple of months of the pandemic, people started harassing me on social media, threatening to report me to the medical board.[44] A tug-of-war between doctors took place on Facebook—sometimes escalating into full-on verbal brawls. Some suggested that somebody needed to go to Houston and shut my clinic down, labeling my practice as "dangerous." I was actually thrown out of most doctor groups on social media because my efforts to wake people up to the truth went against the leftists' crazy new doctrines about what doctors should and should not be allowed to prescribe.

WHY DOCTORS FAILED

Why did doctors fall for this foolishness? I saw several reasons right away. First, most doctors are scared of being sanctioned. Indeed, the law never barred doctors from using hydroxychloroquine. We were just harassed. Even when the FDA gave the recommendation discouraging the use of hydroxychloroquine, it also said that a doctor can always use any medication that has been approved, off label.[45] It was advisory, not a law. But many hospitals took hydroxychloroquine off their formulary, effectively banning it. In my experience if a COVID patient is in the hospital and they don't have hydroxychloroquine on the formulary, the doctors cannot prescribe it even if they want to. That was part of the effort to restrict access to the drug.

Perversely, when the FDA warned physicians against using the drug, it became harder to get pharmacists to fill prescriptions for it. Some states restricted or even prohibited pharmacists from filling off-label prescriptions for it, and some states only authorized it to be given in the hospitals when patients were admitted.[46] Meanwhile, patients were dying.[47]

Another reason it is easy to control American doctors and deceive them is because of the way the American medical system is structured. Most doctors in America are in one specialty or another. There is such a high level of specialization in medicine that only about 30 percent of the doctors with whom people interact on a daily basis are primary care doctors who see COVID patients.[48] A lot of doctors giving opinions—such as Fauci and Gupta—will never be positioned to see a COVID patient. Many of them are from exotic specialties such as immunology, neurosurgery, dermatology, radiology, plastic surgery, and so on. They had no direct experience with COVID patients. None.

Perhaps most discouraging is that many doctors worked for institutions whose directives had been well incentivized to reward certain treatment options. For example, Medicare paid an extra 20 percent to hospitals for COVID patients, so hospitals could get paid more than $10,000 for COVID admissions, and if a patient was intubated, that could go up to close to $40,000.[49] So these institutions refused to use hydroxychloroquine and threatened or fired some doctors who did.[50] Media favorably reported on the firings, thus silencing other doctors. As we were threatened by the boards, many physicians became scared of losing their licenses and livelihoods. Then there were the leftist doctors whose hatred for President Trump superseded their Hippocratic oath.

Others just didn't want to be sued. I was quite comfortable with the quinolines, so I did not fall for the "Hydroxychloroquine will kill you" lie, but many doctors didn't know better and were scared of being sued if those claims turned out to be true. They believed the propaganda without doing their due diligence on the drug.

It all added up to one result: as a body the medical community failed the people. Many doctors had become "good Germans," a reference to those who "went along to get along" in Nazi Germany in the 1930s. Worse, some doctors came to me for prophylaxis and treatment but were too scared to treat their patients with the same regimen.

Chapter 6

JUST BEING A DOCTOR

B Y MAY OF 2020 the virus had hit Houston hard and patients were coming into my clinic with oxygen saturations of 80 percent (which is very low) and shortness of breath. But because our whole staff was taking hydroxychloroquine, there was a great deal of peace in our office. When people walked in, we didn't treat them like they had the bubonic plague. We were not fear driven in the least. Rather, we smiled and told them, "Welcome. It's going to be OK." When appropriate we hugged them. By now we were no longer wearing our big space suits, snorkeling goggles, and shoe covers but only little surgical masks. We had thrown off the COVID costume, which had only engendered fear in our patients without providing meaningful protection. This allowed us to serve people as people, and it was extremely rewarding to see the lives we were saving.

Word got around that we were treating COVID patients, and while our regular patients mostly stayed away, COVID patients came from great distances, some driving four hours to see us. "We've got you; don't worry, you will be fine," we told them. They had all sorts of risk factors: obesity, diabetes, COPD, advanced age. We gave them breathing treatments, IVF, banana bags, hydroxychloroquine, and ivermectin cocktail. We "prophylaxed" their family members and contacts, assuring them that there was no need to hide from the infected person. People came back to us crying for joy that they were alive, and they brought their friends and relatives for treatment.

One lady came to us after signing her eighty-year-old father out of the hospital. She drove three hours to get to us and said her mom had died of COVID the week before.

"I will do everything I can to keep my father alive," she said. He was sick and short of breath, and we treated him, and he is alive and well today.

We had a case of a young lady from my country. She wasn't my patient, but she was sick with COVID—and seven months pregnant. She had gone to the hospital, and they gave her antibiotics for the pneumonia and told her to go home and take Tylenol. Her husband came to see me, and we treated him. Her mother-in-law got sick, and we treated her. They then told me that the daughter was at home, suffering. The whole family was helpless, paralyzed by fear.

I met with the young mother via video conference, and she was so short of breath she could barely talk.

"You need to rush her to our clinic," I told them, and they were desperate enough to overcome their fears and do it. They practically carried her in because she could not walk for shortness of breath. We gave her Decadron, a DuoNeb breathing treatment. We gave her a Rocephin shot and a dose of hydroxychloroquine. Her breathing improved instantly. We sent her home with Cefzil, Z-Pak, hydroxychloroquine, and vitamins. Within forty-eight hours she was better. Within a week she was back to cooking and taking care of her family.

A week later she came bouncing through the clinic to thank us. Her mom kept saying, "Thank you, Doctor. We sat there daily, watching her get worse, knowing she was going to die.

Doctor, do you know how it feels to watch your baby and unborn grandbaby die slowly in front of you? The fear, Doctor, the fear!" But now she kept saying as well, "Thank you, Doctor, and thank you, Jesus."

I told her story to some other doctors online, and a doctor who works in a hospital said, "It is so sad. I'm an OB. I had the same type of patient, about twenty-eight years old, who was eight months pregnant and had COVID. I begged the hospital to give her hydroxychloroquine, and they refused. As I'm talking to you, they had to cut her baby out of her and she's on a heart-lung machine. I don't think she's going to make it." Stories like this were simply heart-wrenching.

I treated one man from Minnesota via telephone. He weighed 350 pounds and was diabetic. He called me that day crying, saying, "Dr. Stella, I don't want to die!" Many doctors would have concluded, "What is the chance that a fifty-something-year-old man who is morbidly obese and diabetic can survive COVID?" But I told him, "Don't worry." We called the pharmacy near him, and of course the pharmacy was playing the part of the police, harassing us and not wanting to fill prescriptions.

"We're not going to fill it," the pharmacist told me.

"What's your name?" I asked, and she gave it to me.

I said, "Right now, as I'm talking to you, there's a 350-pound man in his house, a COVID-positive diabetic, scared that he's going to die. If he does die because you did not fill his prescription, I will sue you and [the pharmacy] for everything that you have—and that I promise you."

I hung up the phone. There must have been something in my voice that scared her, because she immediately called the patient and told him to please tell me to call back and give the prescription again. I did, she filled it, and the man lived.

Some people, especially Africans, would only call me when they or their family members became sick, and the reason they delayed is because I was a Trump supporter and they didn't want to listen to me. But when they got sick, some family member would text me in the middle of the night, asking, "Dr. Stella, what do we do? What do we do?" We did the same thing we did for everyone else. I told them, "Don't worry, we've got you. We will take care of you."

Many, many people came to my clinic after suffering mistreatment and coercion at hospitals. Because of the hospitals' extreme, illogical protocols, hospitals had become prisons of death. Instead of giving people comfort, hope, and choices for care, they terrified people with their ridiculous demands and policies. Many Americans died because they refused to go to the hospital for other diseases because hospitals were testing everyone for COVID and demanding they check into the hospital to receive any treatment whatsoever, even if their problem had nothing to do with COVID.

One family friend brought his wife to the hospital because she was having vertigo. They checked her for COVID, claimed she had it, and insisted on admitting her to the hospital. When she refused, they would not even give her a prescription for vertigo because she had signed herself out against their medical advice. I prayed for this couple and gave her a simple prescription for vertigo.

It happened several times that families basically ran away from hospitals that were trying to force them to be admitted. They knew they would be separated from their loved ones and at the mercy of the hospital's crazy COVID protocols. These patients, who were often very sick, showed up to my clinic.

Half of them could hardly breathe, and some appeared ashen and ready to collapse.

"We are not an emergency room. You can't come here," I told them in the beginning, and they responded, "Dr. Stella, if you don't see us, we are just going to go back home and die." What do you do when somebody is standing in front of your clinic, you see their clinical situation, you know that they should be in an emergency room, not your clinic, and they are telling you, "If you don't treat me, I'm just going to go back home and die"? You treat them.

I could not turn my clinic into a place to receive all emergency patients, but our hospital system had failed people, and as it turned out, God had prepared me by having me work in emergency rooms for many years. We usually gave these people breathing treatments, an antibiotic, and hydroxychloroquine. Sometimes we gave them IV fluids if they were dehydrated. Then we would tell them, "Now go to the emergency room. That one dose of medicine will protect you because hydroxychloroquine lasts in your system for almost a week. When you leave here, go first to the pharmacy, fill your prescription, and put it inside your bag so you can continue taking your hydroxychloroquine in the hospital."

That was how we dealt with the desperate strangers who showed up begging to be treated. They came because they knew we would take care of them, and we did.

But sometimes they didn't take our medical advice.

A forty-something-year-old man from another state saw us via telehealth, and we put him on hydroxychloroquine. He was obese, diabetic, and afflicted by sleep apnea and asthma. He was one of the patients who was too scared to go to the hospital because he feared dying alone. We did the best we could with him, but two days later he got pneumonia and was growing steadily worse. We urged him to go to the emergency room.

"No way," he said. "If I go to the emergency room, Dr. Stella, they're going to lock me up in that hospital and I will die without seeing my family."

I prayed with him that day and told him, "Please, go to the emergency room. You are already on hydroxychloroquine. You're going to be OK. Go to the emergency room. At least they will give you oxygen; they will keep your levels up."

But he refused to go. A day later I called to check on him, and his wife said he had passed away in the house, no longer able to breathe. By the time the ambulance came, they could not revive him. That man could have been saved, but he preferred to die at home rather than risk dying alone in a hospital that nonsensically refused to let his loved ones in.

The same thing happened with the first patient I lost, a ninety-two-year-old diabetic woman. I had treated four other people in her household, including two people in their seventies. All had been sick. When the old woman began having diarrhea, I instructed her, "Please, have your family take you to the emergency room so they can give you fluids to keep you from being dehydrated."

She replied, "No, my husband died last year. I'm not scared to go be with Jesus. I am definitely not going to that hospital, where I will never see my family again."

They even tried to come give her an IV at home, but she refused and eventually died.

Thankfully, the number of bad outcomes was minuscule compared with the hundreds of people being made well by these simple treatments. I became convinced that fear was killing more people than COVID was! At least it seemed that way out there on the front lines.

One young Hispanic man came to the clinic having tested positive for COVID, and while we were checking him in, he abruptly turned, walked to his car, and drove off. At that time, fear was so rampant that some people actually drove to our clinic in their cars wearing full Tyvec suits! This man was not one of them, but apparently his sister had called from another state and said the medicine we wanted to give him was banned and dangerous and could stop his heart. I'm not sure he ever received treatment, because he never came back.

One woman tested positive and went to her doctor, but when she walked in and said she was COVID-positive, everybody in the clinic put on double masks and treated her as if she had leprosy. She then came to my clinic, and everyone was so caring and personable that it made all the difference. Our staff took her and her family into a room, gave them a breathing treatment, and took care of them. She texted me later to say how nice my staff had been to her and her family, welcoming her and treating her without being in any way afraid.

At the height of the COVID crisis, a lot of people came to me, asking what doses I was using. It was a busy period. I put together my protocol and gave it to a lot of people. I shared it with doctors' groups online, and it was an honor to do so. There were doctors with more letters behind their names than I could count, but they came to me to get treated. They would argue about it, but when they got sick, they called, and I was honored to treat them. By being so vocal and unafraid, I became the consultant for doctors and patients alike.

In May, with a big surge of cases in Texas, our clinic was jam-packed with patients. We had opened a pediatric clinic just before COVID hit, and now we converted that clinic to all ages so we could dedicate our main clinic exclusively to COVID patients. By now I had treated more than two hundred COVID patients, and not one of them had died. People found us on Facebook and by referral and came to us from all over Texas. In all that busy time I never got sick because I was on hydroxychloroquine, vitamin D, and zinc. Two of my staff members got sick because they weren't taking the medicine, but we treated them and they recovered.

We were taking care of patients and seeing immediate results. Within a day they were better. Within two days they were often much better. We saw this result over and over.

BANDING TOGETHER FOR GOOD

Online I continued my campaign to convince people that there are effective treatment options that may greatly reduce the risk of dying from COVID. I shared my treatment protocol freely and widely with medical colleagues. I even was honored to send them our extra personal protective equipment when they needed it, because we had stocked up on so many items. But it was becoming increasingly obvious there was something very strange, even sinister, going on in the medical community's refusal to listen to our successes. My heart broke when I heard of people dying when I knew, generally speaking, my protocol might give many people a stronger chance of recovery.

I started connecting with other doctors who were treating patients with these same drugs and supplements and were having the same puzzling experience of knowing these medications work while experiencing significant blowback from medical institutions and colleagues. We began to talk to each other and share data and experiences. Then we started gathering and meeting online, strengthening our relationships and our treatment approaches, and considering how to move forward in a more deliberate and effective way. A number of doctors I met in that crucial time and I have become fast friends.

I met Dr. Richard Urso, also from Houston, on Twitter, and we were so excited to hear from each other because it was such a lonely road when fighting the battles alone. The medical board was coming after him for his stand.[1] We talked by phone for half an hour or more, though we both were busy. It was so encouraging to share thoughts with a like-minded physician!

One day I was busy, and Dr. Urso was trying to call me and couldn't reach me. He sent me a text asking if I was OK. At that time, we were being threatened from every direction, and he didn't know whether I had been attacked or arrested, or if perhaps something bad had happened to me. That was the atmosphere of intimidation we found ourselves in just because we wanted to take care of patients.

I then met Dr. Armstrong of Texas City, who had treated thirty-eight patients in a nursing home on the hydroxychloroquine regimen and lost only one at first. (Two more died later on.)[2] He was very excited about the results but was immediately attacked by the media and the Texas board.[3] It did not make any sense. If you heard that somebody treated thirty-eight patients in a nursing home and all but three survived, wouldn't you want to go there and see what he did? Instead, the authorities attacked him, told him he was practicing dangerous medicine, and grilled him about whether he got consent from the families of the patients. Of course he had, because when patients enter nursing homes, the homes get consent from their families before they are admitted.

Dr. Armstrong was interviewed on Fox News, and his

situation got crazier.[4] I was told that at one point even Congress wanted to censure him. Things were beyond bizarre. How is it that a practicing doctor can tell you he treated nearly forty patients and almost all were alive and well and you want to silence him? That was what we were up against.

I also met Brian Procter, who was in McKinney, Texas. Brian wrote a letter that went viral before it was removed from social media.[5] I called him and we started talking as well. Eventually a number of us formed a hydroxychloroquine group. There was a group on ivermectin too, as doctors from Brazil started speaking up about using that drug, which was proving effective.[6]

In or around May, our little, budding coalition got our first break. I will be forever grateful to Texas state senator Bob Hall, an amazing person and one of the first lawmakers to listen to us and give credence to what we were saying. He held a town hall meeting with us that was streamed on Facebook.[7] That town hall meeting received more than a hundred thousand views. On it we talked about our experiences with COVID and how we were treating it. Bob boldly supported us, held meetings to air our views, and wrote letters to the board telling it to back off and stop harassing doctors.[8] The Texas board was proving to be one of the most radical boards in the country, and we were on a collision course with its views. We often wondered how we—or our careers—would survive it, when God, in His infinite mercy, sent several key lawmakers to support us. He doesn't keep you from battle but brings allies to your side and equips you to win!

One of the doctors in our group connected me to a Texas radio talk show host, and when I went on his show, people called in from everywhere. As a result of that exposure, our clinic overflowed with patients coming for treatment. We had to recruit more staff and work long hours, but it was very rewarding to see somebody walk in who could not breathe well, or who was totally terrified by the news reports, and help that person find peace and recover from the virus.

REAL-WORLD RESULTS

Good results weren't just happening in my clinic, or even in America. I tell people all the time to look at Nigeria. COVID came to Nigeria about a month after it entered America.[9] But when people left China for Nigeria, they were encouraged to take anti-malaria medication,[10] usually Malarone. Malarone has atovaquone, which is also a quinone. So it probably knocked the COVID out of them before they got to Nigeria, which is probably why Nigeria did not suffer the wildfire of COVID that other countries did. Melinda Gates predicted that Africans would start dropping like flies,[11] but it didn't happen. You cannot social distance in the slums of Ajegunle in Lagos, Nigeria. So why did COVID not ravage Nigeria as it did the United States? It could have decimated the country before the people even realized it was there, because many Chinese travel in and out of Nigeria, but when COVID made its way to Nigeria, it did not spread. Why?

When people get a cough or fever in Nigeria, as in many other parts of sub-Saharan Africa, they go to the store and buy malaria medicine. They take it and get well. Sub-Saharan Africa has been spared because it is a malaria endemic zone. People get malaria medicine over the counter in many countries. As of July 3, 2021, the total confirmed cases of COVID in Nigeria as reported by the World Health Organization was 167,618, while the death toll was 2,120. That means only 0.08

percent of the population got COVID, while in the United States more than 10 percent of the population got it. Nigeria's death rate of those who contracted the virus was also lower than the rate in the United States, 1.2 percent, compared with 1.8 percent.[12]

At the time of this writing, there are almost 97,000 COVID deaths in the whole of Africa, 63 percent of which were in South Africa.[13] Malaria is not endemic in South Africa, with only 10 percent of the population at risk of contracting it, and medicines such as hydroxychloroquine are not gotten over the counter, just like in America.[14] South Africa has more of an "American" medical profile, if I can put it that way. But in many other parts of Africa, they are taking hydroxychloroquine and ivermectin and people are living.[15] There are locations in Brazil that started using ivermectin, distributing doses to the populations of several cities, and the number of new cases declined significantly, as did mortality rates.[16]

The same kind of numbers were coming out of India, with only 2.2 percent of the population contracting the virus,[17] and other countries that have hydroxychloroquine over the counter.[18] This global data stares you right in the face and screams one conclusion: Western political leaders and medical practitioners have failed their nations. Their governments have turned against their people. This was one of the greatest heartaches we felt as we realized what was happening.

GOING ON OFFENSE

It hit me during that time that this conflict was not about science; it was about controlling people. We were in a diabolical propaganda battle whose ultimate goal was to enslave and rob people of medical freedom, plus all other freedoms. The people opposing us were not just misguided or misinformed—they were practicing evil and getting away with it. It didn't matter how much we tried to tell people the truth; they would not listen. Studies were coming in from all over the world, more than two hundred of them showing that hydroxychloroquine works.[19] Every one of them was knocked down on social media and other online sites. When Dr. Risch from Yale and Dr. McCullough actually went for a Senate hearing and tried to give facts, it still did not change anything.[20]

So I told my colleagues, "If you all are going to be Mr. Nice Doctors, you can count me out. This has to stop. You cannot come into a street fight wearing a suit." I and others decided we would go on the offensive. We would push back on leftist doctors and their misleading propaganda. We would fight back and hit hard. If I was attacked, I tagged others, and we descended on the perpetrator with fury. We shared notes and strategies and became like brothers and sisters in the biggest fight of our careers, and maybe our lives.

If on Facebook I saw doctors saying, "Hydroxychloroquine doesn't work," I pursued them with questions, asking, "What's your problem? Are you *trying* to kill people? What do you mean it doesn't work? Have you ever given somebody hydroxychloroquine? What is wrong with you? You know this thing works; you want people to die; are you diabolical? Are you Satan's child?"

I threw all kinds of words at them. I remember one big-name doctor who wrote an article saying hydroxychloroquine doesn't work. I went after him until he took down his article. In our exchanges, he said, "I take care of patients. I teach medical students." I replied, "Just like I would tell medical students: sir, take your eyes off the textbook and look at the patient. When was the last time you saw a patient who couldn't breathe?" It was one of a number of skirmishes I won by dogged persistence.

By being openly hostile to anyone who opposed hydroxychloroquine, I earned a reputation as an attack dog. I attacked because every other method was not working. I went on Twitter and said, "Sanjay Gupta, you are a neurosurgeon, what business do you have with primary care? Have you ever even seen a COVID patient?" It did not stop CNN and CNBC from going on an all-out war against the drug.

I went after the *Lancet* study, which had used faulty data but which was covered in the news as valid. I went after the Minnesota University study showing hydroxychloroquine could not be used for exposure to the virus even though they waited four days after exposure to the virus before starting some patients on the drug, giving ample time for the disease to take hold.

How could anyone expect us, as doctors seeing patients survive and thrive because of our "controversial" treatment, to be quiet and let people die? COVID doesn't care whether you are Black or White, Democrat or Republican. Lives and economies have been indiscriminately destroyed because people have rejected knowledge about this virus and its treatment. The media became the willing and eager propaganda machine. YouTube, Facebook, and others became enthusiastic censors, deciding which information was "false" or "dangerous." Facebook later overturned a decision to ban a post about hydroxychloroquine,[21] but people had already died.

That was the battle we were fighting. There was no way we were going to lose it. Then, suddenly, the stage got bigger and our cause went global. I went from my practice in Houston to the steps of the US Supreme Court—and into my God-given destiny.

Chapter 7

JOURNEY TO THE SUPREME COURT

S ENATOR HALL, AFTER our second Zoom Town Hall,[1] started a small COVID-19 task force group, which did a lot to connect and empower doctors who were challenging the medical narrative about COVID treatments. More people came to my clinic seeking help. As our doctor group grew, so did our courage. We all knew something was off. We continued to raise our voices to wake up doctors online, but many were not listening.

Dr. Richard Urso went to a meeting in DC, met a lot of lawmakers, and was on the *Laura Ingraham Show*.[2] Laura was one voice that continued to promote the efficacy of hydroxychloroquine. By now the president was mute because of the media's coordinated plan to silence him. Dr. Urso also brought back news of a new group that had formed.

"Stella, there's going to be a meeting in DC," he told me. "They have another conference coming up. I'm telling you, you need to come. You need to come."

I didn't know what the meeting was about. A month before this I had gotten connected to what I came to know as America's Frontline Doctors (AFLDS). I think it had to do with a tweet I sent. One day I became so frustrated I sent out a tweet saying, "I refuse to be caged by fake science, I have treated over 300 patients with Hydroxychloroquine and [azithromycin] and zinc and not lost any. All those studies saying it does not work is faked science paid for by big pharma." The tweet instantly became a sensation, and I went from one thousand to eight thousand Twitter followers in forty-eight hours. As people shared it, some asked, "Who is this woman? She needs to be part of the Frontline Doctors. She needs to come to DC with us."

That's how I met Dr. Simone Gold, founder of America's Frontline Doctors, which was putting together a meeting. We talked, and I was blunt with the group: "We cannot keep on 'patty-caking' this. I know you guys want to sound like the responsible doctors you are, but truly, I'm done fighting this so-called science battle because all of this has no science to it: the masking, the lockdowns. A two-week lockdown to flatten the curve became a forever lockdown! It went from 'flattening the curve' so we don't overwhelm the hospitals to 'Every COVID case must be gone before we open up.'"

I had crossed a threshold. I was done playing Miss Nice Doctor. People were dying, and all these three-letter medical institutions, with the backing of the media, Big Tech, and the Democratic Party, were playing Russian roulette with American lives. It was not funny. I had decided I would do whatever I could to stand for people—and if I perished, I perished.

I decided to go to DC to attend the conference but had no idea what would come of it.

In some way I had a sense that I was going into the lions' den, and before I headed to the nation's capital, I told my family that things might get dicey out there. If I didn't make it back, it was OK, but I could not let Americans die. I was a

Christian and a minister of the gospel. What would I say when I got to heaven—that I was too scared to stand up, so I let the devil win? This was especially true since the Lord had given me many visions and revelations to show this was a spiritual battle at its root.

Some people still saw COVID as a physical or scientific battle. My conversations with the Lord and the dreams He had given me, plus my knowledge of Scripture and the end-time, told me otherwise. This was something much bigger, with layers so deep that most people's minds would be blown to realize just how evil and deep they were. It had nothing to do with science, which was being used as a front and a tool of control and manipulation. At bottom, this was and is a spiritual battle, a literal good-versus-evil struggle. It involved self-appointed oligarchs who thought they could control the world and some of whom wanted to control governments so they could depopulate the world. This type of plan goes beyond human thinking—it represents an ancient, otherworldly evil with deep roots in our fallen history. The Bible speaks about great evil being loosed on the earth in a time when men try to reject God entirely. For some people, this amounts to crazy talk, but for Christians informed by the Bible, the unfolding scene was familiar because we read about such things in the Word of God.

I went to DC in the identity the Lord had established in me, as a prayer warrior, God's battle-ax, and a trained deliverance minister. I see things from the perspective of a warrior, not a pew warmer, and I know that Christians are the only group of people on planet earth to whom God has given the authority to fight against evil. The battle can only be won by the church. Jesus said in Luke 10:19: "Behold, I give unto you power to tread on serpents and scorpions, and over *all* the power of the enemy: and *nothing* shall by any means hurt you" (emphasis added). To win this battle requires much more than a group of freedom-loving doctors gathering together to stand against governments, as noble as that is. It requires spiritual power and the exposure of evil agendas. That was in my mind as I prepared to fly to DC.

I also had a righteous sense of compassion, which Jesus had when He healed the sick. Each time I heard that thousands more had died of COVID-19, it pierced my soul because I am a doctor and called to help restore life to people's bodies. This didn't have to happen. There are ways people can protect themselves from this malevolent disease, and there are treatment options that I have seen work again and again.

The weekend before I left, I had worked in Louisiana, where I used to do my emergency practice. I told the nurses, "I'm going to DC next week. I don't know what's going to happen, but you all pray for me because if I perish, I perish. But this is not going to continue."

I called my spiritual parents, who happened to be in Florida at the time. I told them, "I'm going to DC, and I'm going to speak up. If I perish, I perish. If I don't come back, so be it. I'm not going to let Americans die."

Maybe you have come to a place in life where you were willing to lose everything for something you believed in. That's where I was in my heart. I was willing to die for this cause, to speak up and face whatever professional or even legal reaction came against me.

I was ready.

D-DAY

The White Coat Summit that Simone had put together was a training program that brought together several doctors to give lectures on topics of interest. It was recorded to be put on America's Frontline Doctors sites. We all took turns at the podium, and I was in high spirits and generally going on the offense and having fun. "Influencers" and members of the media hung around, and we all did several interviews with various media outlets.

That afternoon, we walked over to the Supreme Court. There were not many people there. A few protesters came, including a White dude on a bike adorned with BLM stickers. He was there to heckle us. Before we began speaking, I took the opportunity to heckle him instead. He actually told me that though he was White, he was Black on the inside. I laughed out loud and poked fun at him until he hurried away. I was most definitely in street fight mode.

The modest little press conference began, and Dr. Gold and the two men, Rep. Norman and Dr. Bob Hamilton, spoke before I did. I knew I was in the right place, walking in the grace of God, but I honestly did not realize that what seemed like all of heaven was standing by to amplify what I was about to say. Only God knows when moments like this will happen, which is why we should always be prepared for them. No man or woman can plan such a thing or force it to happen. We can only walk with the Lord and recognize what He is doing, just as Jesus did only what He saw the Father doing.

Of course, as a prayer warrior, I was praying constantly before I took the mic, "Father, give me a mouth and wisdom. When I open my mouth, Lord, speak through me. The righteous are as bold as lions!"

I thought of the world, caged in fear by fear-mongering politicians and "scientists." I saw the whole globe locked up in a prison of terror. The thought "We are all going to die" tormented many people's minds. Plenty of people had not left their homes since March. Many doctors and many citizens had never heard of the treatment protocols using hydroxychloroquine that I and many others had been using against COVID-19. Now God would strike a blow against deception, to restore hope and break fear off of the nations.

I stepped forward at Dr. Gold's invitation and stood there a moment to survey the scene in the natural and in the spirit. Then I raised my voice and began to speak.[3] The message poured out of me. I told all who would listen that Fauci was lying, that we needed a urine sample from him to prove he was not on hydroxychloroquine.[4] I pointed out that CNN's Sanjay Gupta was a neurosurgeon, and what did he know about COVID? I had treated people with diabetes, elderly people with COPD, and hundreds more and had not lost any. I gave these suffering people hydroxychloroquine, azithromycin, and zinc, and they got better. I was there to declare that I would not let Americans die without hearing the truth about this virus and its treatment. If this was the hill I, or my career or my reputation, died on, then so be it. I would not turn back.

I stepped back, and the conference continued, with each doctor speaking more boldly than the one before. Together we shamed and exposed the medical establishment and political leaders for keeping Americans from vital treatments. It was as if God orchestrated our words.

When it ended, much truth had been spoken and revealed, and one of the more enduring images from that conference was the feisty Black lady, anointed by the Holy Spirit, whose voice rang out through the nations, proclaiming that the world is not powerless against COVID. When I opened my mouth and spoke that day, I could feel the Holy Spirit anointing and amplifying my voice in a supernatural way. I had all the boldness of the righteous, and I roared my message like a mighty lioness.

I knew my words shot through the atmospheres of the nations of the world, cutting through the darkness like a beam of concentrated, liberating light. I could feel things break in the spirit realm as I spoke. Hope had dispelled some of the fear. It had thrust a wedge into the enemy's wall of deceit, and the more we pushed on that wedge, the more that wall would come down.

Not only did the clip of me speaking go viral; it went mega-viral. As fast as demonic Big Tech was pulling it down, it was reloaded on other platforms. My words were translated and subtitled in languages all over the world. Finally, the world had found a ray of hope, a better path—a treatment for a virus and for people's fears. The Lord was doing something wonderful for humanity.

Presidential Attention

After the press conference, we went back to the hotel, and I had no idea what the result of our little event would be, because I don't watch TV in hotel rooms and I watch very little at home. For that reason, I didn't see what God was already doing with my voice and the voices of those other brave doctors.

Then my phone rang. It was one of the doctors in our group.

"Stella, we already have four million views," he said.

Four million views? I was shocked. How could four million people have found our video so fast? The answer was, everybody on the internet was sharing it all at once. Then Dr. Urso called me.

"Don Jr. retweeted you," he said, meaning Donald Trump's son. He had retweeted my specific message, which someone had already made into its own clip. I was floored. Then, shortly after that, the president of the United States himself tweeted my clip.[5] *Flabbergasted* is too mild a term for how I felt. The Lord had given me a message to say, and a heart and a platform to say it with, and now He was sending it to the far ends of the earth—and putting it on the lips of the most powerful people.

Of course, darkness was terrified and social media outlets scrambled to censor and squash the message. But you can't contain light in a bottle. God had a message to give to humanity, and nobody could stop it.

Things proceeded quickly. That night, I was told to be ready to attend a meeting with Vice President Mike Pence and other doctors from our group the next day. That morning, staff from my clinic told me that many people had gathered in front of my clinic back in Houston, some of them reporters, some looky-loos, some interested in treatment, and still others there to curse me and what I stood for. (When people you've never met go after you with such vitriol, you have to wonder who their master is!) I was thankful I had planned to be in DC through the end of the month and could miss at least the initial eruption of craziness on my own doorstep.

CANCELED BY THE LEFT, SHUNNED BY THE RIGHT, IGNORED BY CHRISTIAN MEDIA

Also on my phone that morning were calls and texts from family and friends, some concerned, some scolding, others jubilant. I learned that the clip of me had aired on CNN, CNBC, FOX, and many other news channels. Twitter actually suspended Don Jr. for tweeting my video,[6] Madonna called me her hero, and Hollywood descended on her like wolves. Instagram labeled the post false information.[7] Many normal citizens were censored, given warnings, and suspended from Facebook, Twitter, YouTube, and elsewhere for the "crime" of uploading or sharing my video. Amazing.

That day, doctors from our group met with some senators, and I was going along in good spirits, as usual. Then I noticed members of the group whispering, and without being told, I knew something was up. A doctor friend in California called me with a hint of what was to come.

"Stella, you need to take down your ministry YouTube channel," she said.

"Why?" I asked.

"You have been preaching some weird stuff," she said. I just laughed and said, "No way."

Then Dr. Urso came over to me.

"Stella, just be you," he said, but I did not understand the context. Others in our group were fidgeting and giving me funny looks when finally someone spoke up: "Stella, there's a problem."

"What's the problem?" I asked.

"You need to take down your ministry website," she said.

"Are you crazy?" I responded. "Do you know how I came here? Jesus brought me here, and you want me to take down Jesus? You've lost it."

"Demon sperm is trending online," she said.

"What's demon sperm?" I asked.

"You preached a message on demon sperm," she said. "Demon sperm is trending online."

"So let demon sperm trend online," I said. "What's the big deal?"

"It's taking away from the plan," she said. "It's no longer about hydroxychloroquine; it's about demon sperm."

Demon sperm. I saw the enemy's strategy—to boil my whole ministry and medical career down to an out-of-context term I had used while explaining spiritual realities to people in my church. I was neither ashamed nor sad—I was irritated. These people were messing with the power of God, because it wasn't me that planned what God did at the press conference. Clips of our message did not go viral because of our great eloquence. They went viral because God opened the heavens and amplified our voices. I had been praying for this nation for years, pouring out my life and soul for a great harvest of salvations and deliverances. Now was my time of promotion, but these colleagues—good, honest people—wanted me to shut down the ministry side of who I was? That was like turning our backs on God, who had elevated this conference to a global level. All I could tell them was, "Back off."

In that heightened moment of tension, we were able to calm down and continue the meeting we were in, but all was not well. Together our group had bemoaned the cancel culture that silenced our medical message. Now members of that group were urging me to censor myself—or they would cancel me for fear of losing credibility. It wasn't enough to say, "I disagree with Stella on some of her teaching, but we are completely united in our convictions about hydroxychloroquine and how the treatment of this virus is being mismanaged." For some reason, it was all or nothing. I had to repudiate or hide some of my teaching, or apparently I would be disowned.

For the first time on that big of a stage, I felt what it's like to take hits from all sides. The left-wing media was bashing me personally, plus my ministry and beliefs. The media had watched enough of my messages to pull out certain phrases—"demon sperm" chief among them—to attack and ridicule. Conservatives drew back from me as well. Someone reached out to me and asked for my contact information so she could coordinate my appearance on *Hannity* that evening. She came back a few minutes later to say it was not going to be possible. Canceled!

I was supposed to go to the White House to see Vice President Pence. Canceled! I had been interviewed by Breitbart, Turning Point USA, and other conservative media outlets. Those interviews never aired. Canceled!

That evening, I watched as my videos were played on Tucker Carlson while he asked questions of other Frontline Doctors. My image remained on the screen while they spoke, but I was not invited to be on the show. It seemed as if my face was everywhere on the media, in the form of the clip from the press conference, but none of the shows—not Laura Ingraham, not Tucker Carlson, not Sean Hannity, all supposed opponents of cancel culture—would speak with me. They were afraid of being associated with "demon sperm."

So the enemy tried to shift the topic from my claims about treatment with hydroxychloroquine and get friends and foes alike to focus on my ministry and my faith. The emerging narrative about me was clear: I was portrayed as a crazy African woman who believed in weird spiritual things no sensible person would believe in. Anderson Cooper led the charge in ridiculing me and my beliefs. This was the same network, CNN, that had covered Sanjay Gupta doing a weird ritual of washing evil away in a river in India, presenting it approvingly as his religion.[8] When Anderson Cooper ran a story on Bob Larson doing exorcisms, it was apparently worth a whole show.[9] A White guy casting out demons was newsworthy, but a Black immigrant lady talking about demons was a crazy witch doctor. With the other side of his mouth, he and many others proclaimed with a straight face that Black lives matter, women matter, and immigrants matter—except for a successful Black doctor standing against Big Pharma and its diabolical plan.

Former vice president Joe Biden called me crazy,[10] The *Daily Beast* posted several articles about my messages.[11] CNN played clips of my message on incubus and succubus and tried to make fun of it.[12] Interestingly, God redeemed this mockery when many who experienced these things rushed to watch the messages and were delivered! Many wrote comments testifying of their deliverance. These were among the vile comments left by internet trolls.

Sad to say, Christian media treated me much the same way. Popular shows interviewed doctors in America's Frontline Doctors who were not even Christians, and of course they talked about me and put my image on the screen, but they never talked to me. People told me, "We saw you on Fox and all these Christian shows and channels," and I told them, "I've never been on Fox or any of those Christian shows. They wanted to use my face and my voice, but they were afraid to talk to me."

Even some of the members of the Frontline Doctors made statements such as, "Stella, I'm cool with you," or similar things. To be honest, it felt accommodating, like the "one Black friend" kind of comment. Those who have experienced that kind of "friendship" know what I'm saying.

President Trump, true to who he is, supported me without ever knowing or meeting me.[13] In fact, his campaign reached out to me to do an op-ed but I was just overwhelmed and dazed by all that was happening. A July 29, 2020, interview titled "Trump Promotes a Doctor Who Has Claimed Alien DNA Was Used in Medical Treatments," between CNN's Kaitlan Collins and President Trump, went like this:

Collins: "Mr. President, the woman that you said is a great doctor in that video that you retweeted last night said masks don't work and there is a cure for COVID-19, both of which health experts say is not true. She's also made videos saying that doctors make medicine using DNA from aliens and that they're trying to create a vaccine to make you immune from becoming religious."

Trump: "I don't know which country she comes from, but she said that she's had tremendous success with hundreds of different patients. And I thought her voice was an important voice, but I know nothing about her."[14]

Mayor Rudy Giuliani was one of the few who was not afraid to interview me.[15] He said he did not care what I believed in; it was about COVID treatment. Praise God for the brave ones! Finally, someone realized I did not go to DC to preach about demons or "aliens" but to talk about COVID treatment.

BIAS AGAINST CHRISTIAN BELIEFS

Keep in mind, many of the people mocking me proudly proclaim that there are seventy-two different sexual orientations or genders, yet they think I'm crazy. Do you see how the world has gone upside down?

And what do personal beliefs have to do with being a doctor? When you make an appointment with a doctor, do you research his or her spiritual beliefs before you go? When you arrive, does the doctor ask you about your beliefs? I'm not saying these conversations would be wrong or inappropriate in some cases, but there is a sense in which we allow professionals to be professionals, no matter their personal beliefs.

One of the few Christian media outlets that did not shun me at that time was *Charisma* magazine, the leading Charismatic Christian publication, which interviewed me.[16] But when Stephen Strang, owner of Charisma Media, which publishes the magazine, called to offer me a book deal, even he said his distributor might balk at carrying the book. Amazing.

Here I was preaching truth, helping heal people's bodies and souls, and praying for the nation. But Christian and conservative companies were scared of their own faith.

I found it interesting how ready people are to attack biblical Christian beliefs while leaving other religions alone. Preaching about demon spirits and their attempts to control humans is totally biblical. Yet journalists immediately dismiss Christians who speak frankly about this reality. Do they attack the beliefs of Muslims, Hindus, or people of most other religions who believe in an invisible, spirit world that interacts with us, for good or for ill? How about Sanjay Gupta, whom CNN fawned over when he dipped himself in water in India to wash away the evil spirits? They never demanded of him, "Sanjay, you are a doctor—how can you believe in this crazy Indian stuff?" They did not tear down his medical credentials based on his personal beliefs. They did not make him look like a lunatic but rather like an educated, culturally sensitive man with fascinating personal beliefs worthy of respect.

Yet they took my personal beliefs and caricatured them in such a way as to try to tear down my medical career and accomplishments. They took my religion and turned it against me to try to destroy my message. They paid no attention to my medical qualifications and my years of service to people's health. They did not check what I was saying medically about treating COVID. They just attacked me personally, in a way they didn't attack the other doctors.

What they didn't realize—but would have, if they had read the Bible—is that when God opens the heavens over you, nobody can cancel you. When He opens a door, no man can shut it. While the media maligned me, the American people loved me.

Within days I went from 8,000 Twitter followers to nearly 180,000 Twitter followers. Overnight I had a huge audience of people to whom I could speak directly. These people fought for me. They attacked the trolls online. When a fight broke out on one of my posts, I just smiled and said, "They've got this." An army was rising to defend the truth—and me.

I could feel the church worldwide, especially saints in this country, praying for me. The American people I was fighting for loved and appreciated me and held me up in prayer. They saw not only a doctor fighting to keep them alive but a prayer warrior and a patriot.

Sadly, African Americans largely rejected me, either because they believed it when CNN called me "Trump's demon sperm doctor" or they were upset that I openly supported Trump. So many in that community died when they could have been treated. Their own politics shut their ears to an effective treatment. But back home in Cameroon, where I was born, and Nigeria, where I was trained, it was a very different story. I heard of one lady who did negative coverage of me, and the masses rose to my defense, so she had to do two retractions!

When God puts you in the spotlight as He did me, suddenly everyone has an agenda they want you to bow to. Frontline Doctors wanted me to take down my patient care and ministry website and apologize for loving Jesus. I wouldn't do it.

Christian media wanted me to be less controversial and avoid certain topics that are clearly biblical.

Fellow Blacks wanted me to stop supporting Trump and align more with their agenda.

Pagans and non-Christians wanted nothing to do with my Christianity.

Sympathetic doctors thought I should stick to hydroxychloroquine and leave out the spiritual stuff.

Antagonistic doctors hated what I said about COVID treatments.

Some Christians thought I should preach faith instead of advocating medication.

Some wanted me to stand for issues such as child trafficking.

Africans thought I ought to advocate more for my home country and continent.

Then there were those who wanted me to change my accent at age fifty so they could understand me better.

My own parents and half of my siblings were proud of me, and the other half thought I should quit speaking up.

Do you see what happens if you listen to any of the factions? You get off course and into some unanointed agenda. You cannot let people pull you one way or another. You stick with God, and He takes you through to victory.

As all of this was swirling, I did what most other Frontline Doctors did not do: I went home to treat patients again. I am a physician, and my whole orientation is toward caring for individuals. So while my doctor friends began traveling around doing speeches, which is all well and good, I came back to Texas to see patients.

BACK TO WORK

When I came back to Houston, the first thing we did was establish the Frontline MDs, a telehealth platform. To me, taking ground for freedom and for the kingdom of God is about more than just talk. You have to offer people a solution. We worked with nurse practitioners and doctors to take care of patients via private videoconferences. We also started a daily prayer program for the nation and committed to praying in the church for two to three hours every day until revival comes.

On the practical side, life would never be the same. We had to hire security at the clinic to stop reporters from coming in. It became a chore to go to the clinic, where every visitor wanted a selfie with me. Because we had started doing telemedicine, I was able to stay in the background a little more. But my days of practicing medicine anonymously were over.

My spiritual parents, Mosy and Gloria Madugba, stayed in my house and were the anchor that kept me steady. There were so many voices talking at that time—pastors telling me to be quiet, family members upset about being caught in the media frenzy, friends and well-wishers all telling me how to handle things. The voices were many, and most meant well, but all that confusion was quelled by the reassuring presence of my spiritual parents. They answered my ministry phone and sifted through the thousands of messages coming in each day. They screened interviews, answered emails, and prayed with me and for me. Daddy Mosy is what I describe as "calm fire." He would tell me to fight back and not back down. He reminded me I was God's warrior princess, that I was trained for this moment.

I would respond with joy, "Yes, the righteous are as bold as a lion. I have been trained for this. I'm a spiritual, cutthroat warrior in the kingdom of God. I'm a general in God's kingdom, and I know my commander in chief. He watches over me." When people say, "You can't just say things that you say," I say, "Oh, yes, I can." It's because I know whom I belong to, and when you are a princess in the kingdom, you go everywhere with royal guards. Wherever I go, the King's angels watch over me—that's a fact.

That is the only reason I have not been silenced—because I am a child of God, a warrior. His grace and hand cover me. I'm the Esther of this generation, a voice God raised up to fight this battle for such a time as this.

Meanwhile, the controversy continued. I was interviewed on *The Alex Jones Show*, and people on the so-called Right who have tried to cancel him for years attacked me.[17] One particular doctor was giving me highhanded reason why I should not have gone on his show. I wrote this and posted online and received much encouragement. The world needs heroes who will stand up to their convictions against all odds.

This was my post:

> The main problem with you guys is, you claim the left want
> to cancel you because they do not agree with you but you
> are trying to cancel Alex because you don't agree with him.
> I bet if you were the one out there, someone will be telling
> me not to talk to you.[18]

I also did an interview with Channel 2 news, knowing they would not be friendly toward me. That day, I decided I was not going to run and hide but fight back even stronger. Most conservatives at some point seem to cower and hide from the leftist maniacs, but I would take the battle to them. Four years of President Trump had taught me that the only way to survive all the criticism was to fight back.

On the Channel 2 interview, I had fun and warned the reporter that if he twisted my words, I would go after him. I told him I would love to spend an hour with those diabolical CNN anchors and cast those reptilians out of them. They would be slithering on the floor as the snakes came out of them. I was having fun with the subject, but I also meant it in a serious spiritual way. I was God's battle-ax and weapon of war. I was a kingdom sniper and scared of nothing. I was not going to stop treating patients with proven medications just because I was scared of Fauci or the FDA, CDC, or medical board. If they came after me, the battle would be on![19] Neither would I back away from what the Bible says about demons and their power to deceive and control people.

That interview reassured many of those who were worried for me around the world. They saw that I was OK, I was a warrior, and God had my back. It also solidified my public reputation as an unapologetic woman of science and the Spirit. Everyone knows that if they bring me to speak, I will preach. People love it when I speak about Jesus at rallies and conferences and sing a gospel song to close. Afterward I spend hours taking selfies with them. These are the people I was fighting for. They love and appreciate me and the Jesus I serve, and that's what matters.

A few months after the Channel 2 interview, Candace Owens gave me the interview that made many people go, "Hmm...

this woman is not crazy after all." For that I am grateful to Candace and Dennis Prager.[20]

The wonderful truth is, I love being with all people, even my political opponents and those who strongly disagree with me. I enjoy people. This is one of the rewards of being in bondage to no man—you are free to love everyone. I can sincerely say that I love humanity, even those who are deceived. I learned a long time ago that we are all fallen creatures to whom God offers His saving grace and mercy. Every person is a little off in one way or another. I don't expect perfection from anyone or from myself, and I don't place anyone on a pedestal, least of all me! I know one perfect person, and His name is Jesus. To Him alone do I submit. Where He sends me, I go. When He stops me, I don't go. He ate with sinners and never sinned. If He gave His life to love people, so will I.

That is the freedom I have. That is what makes me bold and powerful. I cannot be put in a cage by anyone. God alone brought me to prominence for such a time as this because He knew I would proclaim His name and His Word without fear, intimidation, or compromise. He alone has kept me on top against all odds. He watches over and protects me because I am His warrior princess—and I love Him.

Chapter 8

MIXED SEED AND THE COMING DAYS OF NOAH

THE DEVIL HAS been planning to capture and destroy humanity since Adam and Eve were first created. I believe the ferocious backlash against my message on what came to be known as "demon sperm" happened because the enemy's plans were being exposed. If the devil didn't care, he would have shrugged his shoulders and moved on to someone else because my words could not harm him. But instead he came after me hard. It reminded me of the storm that "coincidentally" sprang up when Jesus headed across the Sea of Galilee to deliver a man on the other side from demons. Do you think that storm just happened to rise up when Jesus was on a deliverance mission? Think again. In a similar way, it felt as if people were labeling me as insane, superstitious, and outside mainstream Christian beliefs because I was, and am, a threat to the devil's plans in our generation.

The only problem for them is that my message is totally biblical.

The real problem with Christians these days is that they believe science over Scripture, reason over revelation. So many believers have fallen into the Western mindset that somehow science has conquered all, and science now defines our worldview and even our view of the Bible. This is a very dangerous lie, akin to the lie the snake told Eve in the garden: "Did God really say?" When we rely on science more than Scripture, we arrive at a twisted view of reality—and we remain ignorant of the devil's schemes (which the Bible tells us not to do; see 2 Corinthians 2:11).

An Ancient Plan Still in Our Future

Let me ask you, When did humans discover genetics and the famed double helix of DNA that resides in each cell of our bodies? Would it surprise you that this happened within some of our own lifetimes, in the 1950s? Think about it: for thousands of years people knew nothing about DNA. We didn't even know about cells! People in Charles Darwin's day believed cells were little blobs of jelly rather than individual, self-contained supercomputers, which is what they actually are. Trillions of these ingenious cells make up each of our bodies—but for most of human existence we knew nothing about them.

Who would have dreamed that within seventy years of figuring out what DNA is, scientists would learn to clone pets, create test-tube babies, and discover treatments for viruses based on messenger RNA? We have come a long way very fast in our understanding of the world God created—yet our knowledge of DNA and human procreation is still very shallow compared with all there is to know. We may think we have mastered the universe—and the cell—but we have only glimpsed the complexity of genetic design.

Now consider how long the devil has been at this business of perverting and twisting the DNA God created—a lot longer than we have, for sure. We should not underestimate Satan's capabilities. He is an extremely intelligent spiritual being who has existed for thousands of years, if not much longer. Do we really think he and his fellow fallen angels—hyperintelligent, ancient spiritual beings—are lagging behind us in the race to crack the genetic code? How proud and arrogant can we be? Demons are not goofy, bumbling little ghosts from some Scooby-Doo episode. They are extraordinarily clever, capable, and—yes—scientific beings that are trying to rule the world. This is the clear, mainstream teaching of the Bible.

Let's look at examples from the Bible itself about how demons try to control and destroy what God made to be good. In Exodus we read how Moses confronted Egypt's leader, Pharaoh, and commanded him to let the Hebrews go free from slavery. The only problem was, Pharaoh's own magicians were able to turn sticks into snakes, just as Moses and Aaron did:

> Then Pharaoh summoned the wise men and the sorcerers, and they, the magicians of Egypt, also did the same by their secret arts. For each man cast down his staff, and they became serpents.
>
> —EXODUS 7:11–12, ESV

Tell me, how did these "wise men," "sorcerers," and "magicians of Egypt" create living beings out of dead wood? It tells us it was "by their secret arts." This was not some illusion or vision. In fact, it immediately tells us that "Aaron's rod swallowed up their rods" (Exod. 7:12, NKJV). These were living, physical entities. Have you ever stopped to wonder just how advanced these men must have been in their cooperation with demons to be able to turn staffs into snakes? Notice too that they were snakes—the same form Satan himself took in the garden.

I wonder how many Christians just skip over that passage, yet it teaches us something. Consider what happened at the molecular or genetic level at that moment. Did these magicians have electron microscopes and lab coats and all the equipment available to manipulate DNA? Of course not, but the knowledge and ability to perform this change was coming from somewhere and happening in cooperation with willing people submitted to demonic influences. At the very least, this should alert us to what is possible for people who come under very dark influences.

The fascinating account continues:

> Moses and Aaron did as the LORD commanded. In the sight of Pharaoh and in the sight of his servants he lifted up the staff and struck the water in the Nile, and all the water in the Nile turned into blood. And the fish in the Nile died, and the Nile stank, so that the Egyptians could not drink water from the Nile. There was blood throughout all the land of Egypt. But the magicians of Egypt did the same by their secret arts.
>
> —Exodus 7:20–22, ESV

By now are you wondering just what these "secret arts" were? Whatever they were was powerful enough to turn all the water in Egypt into blood! Pharaoh wasn't impressed by the signs Moses and Aaron performed by God's power because his own demonized "wise men" were seemingly just as advanced. They had learned how to control aspects of the physical universe with their spiritual powers.

WELL-EDUCATED WITCH DOCTORS

Here's a question: Did the devil just decide to abandon that kind of power way back then? Or is it more credible to imagine that he has been building up to a greater level of control over humanity over thousands of years since that time, using control over nature as one of his means? Clearly the Bible gave us these passages as a warning so we would not be ignorant of the enemy's schemes.

Part of our blindness comes from our location in America, where the enemy's strategy is to use reason and reliance on science to deceive us, rather than using raw displays of power. But talk with missionaries to many foreign countries—or those who work in America with very troubled and tormented people—and they will tell you that demons manifest all the time to control whole regions and populations. Open demonic activity is only uncommon in Western, "civilized" countries. In Africa witch doctors are so common that each village or region has one, and the people go to them for everything from health problems to money and relationship needs. These people, and certainly the witch doctors themselves, could easily testify to seeing literal manifestations of demons or demonic power. They take directions from these supernatural beings, which are the foot soldiers of the being the Bible calls "the prince of the power of the air." (See Ephesians 2:2.) Indeed, the apostle John testified that "the whole world lies in the power of the evil one" (1 John 5:19, ESV). Why then do we ignore the devil's role in current events?

The devil has legal access to meddle in every aspect of the planet where humans yield to his control. Does it shock us that he would try to inhabit or twist the very genetics of human beings? These fall under his area of "control," as John wrote. Our own scientists have the power to do things that alarm ethicists, but do we blindly imagine that the enemy is less intelligent and less advanced than we are?

Is it even possible that some university-trained scientists and doctors are simply well-educated witch doctors, cooperating with the enemy just like someone using the dark arts in an African, Asian, or South American village?

Let's continue to learn from Moses' confrontation with Pharaoh. It gets even weirder:

> Then the LORD spoke to Moses, "Say to Aaron, 'Stretch out your hand with your rod over the streams, over the rivers, and over the ponds, and cause frogs to come up on the land of Egypt.'" So Aaron stretched out his hand over the waters of Egypt, and the frogs came up and covered the land of Egypt. And the magicians did so with their enchantments, and brought up frogs on the land of Egypt.
>
> —Exodus 8:5–7, NKJV

Frogs! Did you ever pause to ask yourself, How did these men cause frogs by the millions to appear all over Egypt? Many Christians read this as if it's mythological or just too strange to explain—but brothers and sisters, it is in the Bible for a reason. We must seek to understand these things, not ignore them because they offend our scientific sensibilities.

Notice too that the Egyptian magicians did not care that frogs were released upon the land to plague the people. Instead of using their "arts" to find a way to remove the frogs, they were only interested in demonstrating their power, even if it meant making the lives of people worse. The devil does not care about humanity, and neither do those who partner with him.

In addition to what this passage tells us about the enemy's abilities and strategies, I also find interesting that both frogs and snakes are the forms demons take elsewhere in the Bible. (See Genesis 3 and Revelation 16:13–14.) Is it possible that God put limits on what the enemy could create or fashion out of earthly stuff? Is it also possible that in the end-time those limits are removed so that evil reaches its full measure? These are things to think about.

Finally, God went beyond what the magicians were able to do. Moses and Aaron caused gnats to invade Egypt; then,

> the magicians tried by their secret arts to produce gnats, but they could not. So there were gnats on man and beast. Then the magicians said to Pharaoh, "This is the finger of God."
> —EXODUS 8:18–19, ESV

Game recognize game, as they say. These sorcerers threw in the towel and told Pharaoh that a spiritual power greater than their dark arts was on the scene. But until we take seriously the astonishing things these evil men were able to do in partnership with demons, we will treat this passage like a fairy tale—and misunderstand our own times as well.

WHOSE SEED?

Now let's look at what the Bible says about what we might call "demon seed." When I first began to dwell on these scriptures, they truly troubled me, and I didn't know what to make of them.

"Lord," I asked, "would You show me what these passages mean? Because they sound like they're saying there are people in the land who are not fully human!"

The first scripture that caught my attention on this subject was Daniel 2, which describes an image that Nebuchadnezzar, the king of Babylon, saw in a dream that Daniel interpreted. The statue had a head of gold, a chest and arms of silver, a belly and thighs of brass, legs of iron, and feet of iron mixed with clay. Daniel interpreted what each part of the image represented. Each spoke of a specific world empire. Nebuchadnezzar's

Babylon was the head of gold. The next kingdom, depicted as a silver chest and arms, would be Persia, followed by Greece, then Rome, and then a last kingdom before the Lord Jesus returned to shatter them all and rule perfectly on the earth.

Of interest to this discussion is the last kingdom, the one of clay mixed with iron. Daniel 2:42–43 (NKJV) tells us,

> As the toes of the feet were partly of iron and partly of clay, so the kingdom shall be partly strong and partly fragile. As you saw iron mixed with ceramic clay, they will mingle with the seed of men; but they will not adhere to one another, just as iron does not mix with clay.

The "seed of men" refers to human offspring—and it clearly says that something represented by "iron" will "mingle with the seed of men" but won't combine together well with it. What is this talking about? In the Bible, clay and dust usually refer to humans. This makes sense in light of the "seed of men" term. Iron could, from a historical perspective, mean machines. Iron characterized the industrial age, and it remains perhaps the most important metal today as well. In a literal way, then, God's interpretation given through Daniel may indicate that humans and machines would mingle at the "seed," or reproductive, level. This sounds strange, but then again, we live in strange days when many things are happening that no one in history would have considered possible.

To understand further about the kingdom immediately preceding the Lord's coming, we can go to another passage in the Bible that introduces this idea of mingled seed. The famous and controversial chapter, Genesis 6, tells us that in the days of Noah, the sons of God came and slept with the daughters of men, and together they produced a strange race of beings called Nephilim. Here's how the passage reads:

Now it came to pass, when men began to multiply on the face of the earth, and daughters were born to them, that the sons of God saw the daughters of men, that they were beautiful; and they took wives for themselves of all whom they chose. And the LORD said, "My Spirit shall not strive with man forever, for he is indeed flesh; yet his days shall be one hundred and twenty years." There were giants on the earth in those days, and also afterward, when the sons of God came in to the daughters of men and they bore children to them. Those were the mighty men who were of old, men of renown.

Then the LORD saw that the wickedness of man was great in the earth, and that every intent of the thoughts of his heart was only evil continually. And the LORD was sorry that He had made man on the earth, and He was grieved in His heart. So the LORD said, "I will destroy man whom I have created from the face of the earth, both man and beast, creeping thing and birds of the air, for I am sorry that I have made them." But Noah found grace in the eyes of the LORD. This is the genealogy of Noah. Noah was a just man, perfect in his generations. Noah walked with God.

—GENESIS 6:1–9, NKJV

Many modern translators try to interpret this in naturalistic ways, but it is very difficult to do so. The Hebrew word for these beings in verse 4 is *nephilim*, which means fallen or mighty ones. To reduce these to strong, athletic men is to rob the word of its meaning. The disconcerting fact is that these were a mixture of fallen angels and human beings—mingled seed. Plenty of intelligent scholars acknowledge this. These creatures, taller and stronger than regular humans, seemed genetically engineered to dominate the human race.

They also brought with them a level of evil so great that God chose to shorten people's life spans to a brief 120 years—an almost 90 percent reduction—and to actually destroy all people except Noah's family. This was caused by an extreme form of evil brought about by mingled seed. God "was grieved in His heart" that he had made mankind. Wow! It had to be a cataclysmic event for God to feel such heartache and to do something He has done just once—flood the entire earth and destroy all living creatures except those kept in the ark. It was the presence of corrupted humanity that prompted God to destroy the world at that time. The devil had corrupted some human DNA, and if he could corrupt it all, spreading strange seed throughout the race, then God could not send a Savior born of a woman to redeem humanity. All the human race would be lost.

Note as well that Noah was described as "perfect in his generations." Some very credible scholars believe this means Noah's line and family were unaffected by the corrupted DNA of that era.

It would be one thing if we could tuck this ancient passage away and treat it as irrelevant to our lives. But Jesus Himself referred to Noah's period of history—and stunningly predicted that it would happen again. He said,

> But as the days of Noah were, so also will the coming of the Son of Man be. For as in the days before the flood, they were eating and drinking, marrying and giving in marriage, until the day that Noah entered the ark, and did not know until the flood came and took them all away, so also will the coming of the Son of Man be.
>
> —MATTHEW 24:37–39, NKJV

Notice that marriage represents half of the activities Jesus predicts here. This echoes what we saw in Genesis 6 about Nephilim who "took wives for themselves of all whom they chose." They didn't just bear offspring with the women—they married them! In other words, they followed human conventions, which in some ways looked "normal." This corresponds with Daniel 2:43, which told us there would be mixed "seed." The English Standard Version of the Bible interprets that Daniel verse this way: "As you saw the iron mixed with soft clay, so they will mix with one another in marriage." There's marriage again.

Now ask, Why would Jesus refer twice to marriage in foretelling what the last days of this age would be like? And why would He refer to marriage specifically in the context of the world situation in Noah's time? Jesus never used words carelessly but deliberately, so we would search out other parts of the Bible He intended for us to understand. This is one of them.

As I studied these passages, I had to conclude that in the last days of this age, strange seed would mingle with human seed, creating half-human creatures who would in some ways look and act like humans but who would abound in evil and possess attributes of unusual strength or power. That opens the door, necessarily, to the idea that in some way people of mixed seed are in the land, among us today, or will be in the future.

We don't see literal giants walking around the earth. That would make their presence obvious. But that is not their only characteristic. The Nephilim also have supernaturally evil thought processes. Their every plan and scheme is to warp and twist what God made to be good, just as they themselves are twisted forms of humanity. Do we see a staggering increase in warped, twisted, unimaginable evil on the earth today? Yes, more than ever. What could be more warped and twisted than lawmakers potentially forcing doctors to allow minors to have radical surgeries to "change their sex" without parental permission? What could be more evil? How about the way people try to redefine and confuse every idea associated with gender and sexuality? A regular human mind cannot comprehend the kind of crazy evil we see being promoted in our culture. That is the type of thinking we are dealing with.

The apostle Jude wrote that these Nephilim were punished for their behavior and kept in captivity—until the last days or the last day itself:

> And the angels who did not keep their proper domain, but left their own abode, He has reserved in everlasting chains under darkness for the judgment of the great day; as Sodom and Gomorrah, and the cities around them in a similar manner to these, having given themselves over to sexual immorality and gone after strange flesh, are set forth as an example, suffering the vengeance of eternal fire.
>
> —JUDE 6–7, NKJV

Whether this means that these beings will reappear for a short time leading up to "the great day" isn't clear. But their ultimate transgression was clearly partaking in "strange flesh" with humans. Demons are never content to stay in the spiritual world. They want to control this world. That's why a third of Jesus' ministry on earth was casting demons out of people. These demons caused madness, infirmity, violence, and other things. They wanted to control people and rule the world—and still do.

Is it any wonder that many people who are troubled by demon spirits have dreams that involve lurid and evil forms of sex? Those who minister in deliverance know what I'm talking about and how demons put those thoughts in tormented people's minds.

If you find all this hard to imagine, the Bible itself promises that evil will manifest in all sorts of supernatural and miraculous ways in the days ahead. Those living in these times will see things we cannot imagine. For example, Revelation 13 talks about a leader labeled "the beast":

> He performs great signs, so that he even makes fire come down from heaven on the earth in the sight of men. And he deceives those who dwell on the earth by those signs which he was granted to do in the sight of the beast, telling those who dwell on the earth to make an image to the beast who was wounded by the sword and lived. He was granted *power* to give breath to the image of the beast, that the image of the beast should both speak and cause as many as would not worship the image of the beast to be killed.
> —REVELATION 13:13–15, NKJV

As Pharaoh's magicians had power to give life to snakes and frogs, the beast will have power to give life to this image. He will cause "all, both small and great, rich and poor, free and slave, to receive a mark on their right hand or on their foreheads, and that no one may buy or sell except one who has the mark or the name of the beast, or the number of his name" (Rev. 13:16–17, NKJV).

It takes an extreme, supernatural level of power to cause everyone to obey you. And it begins by giving life to something inanimate, as magicians did in Moses' day.

MINGLED SEED NOW?

Let me draw a parallel with where we are today and allow you to come to your own conclusions.

Have we ever witnessed such a level of global control and exercise of raw power to cause people to conform to a certain agenda as we did starting in 2020? The agenda I refer to is submitting to whatever the government claims about COVID-19 and accepting the vaccines without resistance. What happened when this agenda exploded in our nation? We saw some people resist, but we saw a lot of people go right along with the agenda as if they were robots. Indeed, they behaved like unthinking machines, accepting whatever the "authorities" said. Worse than that, they worked against people who didn't go along with the agenda. As pharmacists, they refused to fill prescriptions for hydroxychloroquine or other treatments. As ER doctors, they refused to see patients who didn't agree to be checked in for COVID-19. As tech workers at Google, Twitter, Facebook, and Apple, they deleted posts about hydroxychloroquine or the devastating effect of lockdowns or stolen elections or anything else not on their global agenda. This happened so quickly and with such uniform obedience from so many that it almost seems supernatural. Could it be?

When professionals such as me scream and make a ruckus about effective treatments for COVID-19, yet governments block those treatments and social media persecutes and deletes those who mention them, what is really going on?

When leaders and medical professionals and legal experts and rulers of entertainment and social media walk in such lockstep to the same agenda, clearly something diabolical is at work. This is the spirit that shuts down churches, stops effective treatments from being given, intimidates those who love liberty, and undermines the foundations of righteousness in society. This is the spirit that says it's OK to rip babies from the womb up to the moment they're born, then exports this sick practice overseas with US government funds.

If this isn't the hallmark of "mingled seed" in the land, then at least it is a form of national possession. There is no other explanation for why people would willingly do such crazy, wicked things in a seemingly coordinated and effective way.

Add to this the fact that the whole pandemic seemed aimed at getting every human to take a vaccine. Actually, it is not a vaccine in the traditional sense at all but a radical new form of human "software." Moderna's vaccine is a messenger RNA, which goes into your system and tells your body to produce certain proteins. I believe this vaccine impacts human genetics and is well down the pathway of rewriting human DNA. The Johnson & Johnson vaccine was developed using aborted fetal cell lines.[1] For several months in Israel, they had internal COVID-19 vaccination passports called Green Passes, which allowed vaccinated citizens access to otherwise restricted places, such as theaters and gyms.[2] We no longer have to wonder what a universal mark that restricts who can and cannot participate in the economy looks like—it's here.

Enormous pressure is being applied by companies and employers to force people to take the vaccine. Many are already losing their jobs, or quitting under pressure, for not giving in.

As I told One America News Network, "I think that the media is just hyping this because they want to sell vaccines. And I would say from the beginning, the whole way they handled everything was a lie....Yes, we do have a disease, yes, it kills people that have some...underlying diseases, but it's not the scary disease that everybody is making it out to be, and it has effective treatment and effective prevention. So I believe some of the hype is because they want people to take vaccines. They want to scare people that are...still resisting taking the vaccine. Really this disease is endemic now and I think we are going to deal with it for a while....The disease is very manageable, it's easy to treat."[3]

I reiterated that people such as me were being censored online by some social media companies. "They are censoring us because we are saying the truth. They don't want to treat people, they want to sell vaccine. I think this whole pandemic was made for the vaccine instead of the other way round and I just wish people would wake up and realize that this is not a Democrat...or Republican issue; it's a humanity issue."[4]

The reporter pointed out that "despite rapidly falling cases of the Chinese virus, the media and Democrats are continuing to hype up the disease and may even force Americans to use a vaccine passport to leave their homes."[5] An article by Husch Blackwell states that "per recent federal employment law guidance, private employers can generally require employees to get vaccinated for COVID-19 as long as they comply with federal employment laws that prohibit discrimination on the basis of religion and disability.

"At the state level, with the increasing availability of the COVID-19 vaccine, a number of states are beginning to consider passing legislation to prevent employers from mandating vaccinations and protect those who refuse vaccinations. This type of pending legislation is at various phases, and at this point no legislation specifically pertaining to refusal of the COVID-19 vaccine has been passed into law."[6]

Meanwhile, doubts are rising about the so-called vaccines. There are reports of serious side effects on people who took them.[7] Denmark banned the use of AstraZeneca "following news of its possible link to very rare blood clot cases," according to Reuters.[8]

Johnson & Johnson's Janssen temporarily halted production of its vaccine. According to the Centers for Disease Control and Prevention, "CDC and FDA are reviewing data involving six reported U.S. cases of a rare and severe type of blood clot in individuals after receiving the J&J vaccine. In these cases, a type of blood clot called cerebral venous sinus thrombosis (CVST) was seen in combination with low levels of blood platelets (thrombocytopenia)....CDC will convene a meeting of the Advisory Committee on Immunization Practices (ACIP) on Wednesday to further review these cases and assess their potential significance. FDA will review that analysis as it also investigates these cases. Until that process is complete, we are recommending a pause in the use of this vaccine out of an abundance of caution....People who have received the J&J vaccine who develop severe headache, abdominal pain, leg pain, or shortness of breath within three weeks after vaccination should contact their health care provider."[9]

We have seen so much since the beginning of 2020 that nobody really dreamed of happening. Would it surprise anyone, least of all Christians who know what the Bible says about the last days, if this whole thing has been about corrupting human DNA? Is the devil using doctors and science to wage war on humanity at the genetic level? What's next? What can we imagine scientists (and politicians) cooking up next to frighten and control huge populations, ultimately convincing (or forcing) them to alter their very DNA with so-called cures meant to keep everyone safe?

The only group that can stop the spread of evil is the church. But the church is sleeping. For years and years, agents of the devil have given money to big preachers and denominations so they stay out of his way. They seem to have made a deal with the devil to preach about the American dream while the god of this world goes about his business.

Even before there was the virus and the vaccines, the devil's fingerprints were all over this generation. Ten years ago, who would have dreamed so many people would be covered by tattoos, addicted to violence, unashamed about watching explicit sex scenes, changing their gender (which is impossible to do), and training our children in schools that they are neither boys nor girls until they decide to be?

Who would have thought that Black children would act as if somebody had enslaved them and attack people who were never slave owners just because of the color of their skin? Who could have foreseen that a government would give so much money in the form of "free" handouts that businesses could not find employees to work for them? Who imagined able-bodied people sitting home on the couch because they made more by not working?

How about the nearly total destruction of the Black family and community and the welfare-addicted inner cities? Friends, we see all around us the evidence of a grand diabolical plan being carried out. When will we realize that unseen forces acting on humanity have built the chaos to this level—and they want to do worse?

Is there mingled seed among us in the land? I believe there is. Even if there isn't, there will be before the end of this age, when the level of demonization will change the face of humanity, quite literally. Lying miracles will abound, treachery and violence will saturate the culture, and we will see for ourselves what it was like in the days of Noah, when evil reached such a crescendo that God wiped out the human race, sparing just eight people. Of course, we know this age will end with the trumpet sound and second coming of our blessed Savior, Jesus Christ, to rule and reign here, seizing all power from the devil and his followers. Then those of us who stood and fought with Him in this age will rise to rule with Him in positions of power prepared for us before the world began. That is our testimony, and by this and the blood of the Lamb we will overcome everything this age can throw at us—engineered viruses, damaging vaccines, and every lie of men.

We will be like Noah was—"perfect in his generations," brought through great storms to be made champions of righteousness, undefeated and undefeatable, mighty to the tearing down of all demonic strongholds.

Chapter 9

WHY DONALD TRUMP IS STILL MY PRESIDENT— AND HOW REVIVAL WILL SWEEP THE GLOBE

W HEN PRESIDENT TRUMP retweeted my video on hydroxychloroquine, many people assumed we had become buddies or even allies. In reality I have never met President Trump and don't know him personally—but I fully support President Trump because I am convinced not only that he is a good leader who means the best for America but that he remains God's choice for America.

My public stand for President Trump delights some people and angers others. Mostly, it surprises people, so let me take a moment to explain why I feel so strongly that President Trump is God's choice to lead America.

Back in 2008 I supported Barack Obama in his first term, but by his second term I found myself disenchanted with some of his ungodly policies. For the first time I began to lean toward the Republican Party. Still on the fence in 2012, I did not vote in that election. I could not see myself voting for such an ungodly man as Barack Obama again. I knew I had been fooled by the color of his skin and his swag. I was in a political wilderness.

Just before the 2016 election I remained a Democrat, and initially when Trump jumped into the race for president, I was not interested in his candidacy. I saw him as nothing more than a Hollywood celebrity. I simply couldn't come to terms with the prospect of an excessive, bombastic billionaire becoming president. Having gradually come over to the Republican Party, I considered giving my vote to Ted Cruz if he won the nomination. He seemed to be a genuine and responsible Christian. But my choice spoke more about what *I* wanted than anything I felt God saying to me. So I decided to stop and ask God who His choice was. Remembering the prophet Samuel and how he almost chose the next king of Israel from among Jesse's sons based on looks and personality rather than the heart of the man, I knew I didn't want to vote based on personal preference or opinion. I genuinely wanted to know whom God wanted in the highest office.

For the next four days I went before the Lord, and on the first day I had a dream about Hillary Clinton that left me feeling oppressed and freaked out. I knew she was into something dark. When I learned about John Podesta, chairman of her presidential campaign, being invited to a "spirit-cooking dinner," I knew for certain we were dealing with agents of darkness.[1] It shocked me and helped me realize I needed to escape from the Democratic plantation right away!

On the second night I had another dream, this time about the hurricane that had flooded our church in 2015. In the dream I was inside the wrecked church building when Melania Trump came to me. I told her about the hurricane and the resulting issues with the church and insurance company, which had refused to pay for damages. She replied, "That's why you should vote for Donald. Donald will take care of the church. Vote Donald Trump—he's going to set up the church."

When I woke up, I prayed to the Lord and asked Him if we should support Donald Trump and if Trump was going to support the church. I wanted to be sure of what I had seen and heard in the dream. The Lord confirmed to me, right there, that Trump was His choice. Because I don't like to disobey God, once He revealed His choice to me, I didn't question it. I trust God above all and recognize Him as my *true* commander in chief!

Nevertheless, before casting my vote in the 2016 election, I went to the Bible to do some research. I wanted to know if there was any precedent for God choosing a "bombastic billionaire" such as Donald Trump to lead a nation. Donald Trump is no Boy Scout, as we all know, and in light of his personal history and shenanigans before taking office, I just wasn't sure he fit the mold of a man of God. Choosing to research the subject was my way of ensuring that any dream or vision from God was backed up by the Scripture.

I opened my Bible and thought of Moses, who believed in God but was brought up adhering to the laws of Egypt. Being raised in the house of Pharaoh, he no doubt worshipped the gods of Egypt at some point. Moses went on to murder a man and then ran away to escape justice and punishment. Yet Moses was God's choice and God's instrument to save the Israelites and lead them out of Egypt.

I also revisited the story of David, who had orchestrated the slaying of his own faithful soldier in order to take the man's wife. Yet God described him as a man after His own heart.

Next I looked at the story of Jehu, a chief commander in the army. Though Jehu wasn't a likely candidate to rule a nation, when he accepted the prophet Elijah's invitation to help him take down Jezebel, a wicked queen who had killed God's prophets, Jehu was soon crowned king.

There was also the story of Pharaoh (an earlier Egyptian ruler than Moses' Pharaoh) who defended Joseph, son of Jacob. Here was another gracious gentile who didn't believe in God but was greatly used by God. King Cyrus was another nonbeliever appointed by God to rule.

The records of these men prove that God is in the business of using unlikely characters to achieve His aims and do great things for His people. Yet unlike some of those men, Trump has a spiritual lineage. His mother, Mary, was born and raised in the Hebrides Islands of Scotland, where a great revival broke out in 1949. Though Mary had come to the United States by that time, the revival shook those nations and the world with dramatic examples of repentance and great spiritual power. Trump visited that island and his mother's girlhood house before he became president. His family hailed from a place God had blessed with one of the great revivals of the twentieth century.

Finishing my research, I was convinced that Trump would do great things for the church, so I began supporting him about six months before the election. I posted on social media what I had seen in the dream, and people attacked me, some even going so far as to rain abuses on me. I was only trying to share what I knew was God's will for our country, but I was vilified. (It wouldn't be the last time!) People called me names, but I stood my ground and declared that Donald Trump would win the presidential election—not because of who he was but because of God's sovereign purpose for his life.

I kept prophesying that Donald Trump would win at a time when many felt he stood no chance of winning. On the day before the election, I reassured my friends yet again that Trump would win. Few believed me. But God is always right, and He had His way. Donald Trump became the forty-fifth president of America, and even though it meant I lost a lot of friends and even church members for supporting him, I stood my ground. What God wants is what I want, regardless of the fallout.

INAUGURATION DREAM

On the day of Trump's inauguration, something special happened while I was taking a nap, between 9:00 and 10:00 a.m. I usually do things before dawn, then rest in the mornings. I had been planning to watch the inauguration but had fallen asleep and had a dream.

In the dream a thick, dark cloud was hanging over the nation. Then the dark cloud receded before a blue sky, which grew and grew, signifying a beautiful open heaven over the entire land. As I opened my eyes and turned on the television, they had just sworn in Trump as the forty-fifth president. Over the next four years, I believe heaven did in fact open over our nation. Prosperity came back, there were jobs and a recovered economy, and people were proud of, and hopeful for, America again. The country was regaining respect in the world and was on its way to becoming "great again" in the global community. That's exactly what President Trump did, which is why I was proud to back him for a second term and why to this day I still consider him my president.

While to some Donald Trump is a braggadocio, even a vulgar man, God sometimes uses unexpected people from unexpected places to achieve His purposes on earth—and for His people. In choosing Donald Trump for both a first and second term, God knew He needed someone "crazy" like Jehu to overturn the system, someone with little to no concern for the status quo, someone with few allegiances and obligations who ultimately could not be bought.

I had another significant dream about President Trump during the COVID pandemic. It was June 2020, when the Black Lives Matter movement was making daily headlines. I couldn't help but wonder, was Jesus on His way right then? The marches and protests were getting so out of hand. I went to the Lord again, as is my habit, to ask Him to show me what was going on.

That night in a dream I saw a beaten-up President Trump. He was beaten so badly that he lay motionless on the ground, and in the dream we thought he was dead. I ran over to a group of people there, and we began praying for him. As the prayers intensified in the dream, Trump got off the ground and stood taller—much taller and much bigger than he is in actuality. Then he got back to work. That was the end of the dream.

That is why no matter what the result of the 2020 election looks like right now, I fully believe President Trump will get back to work in a bigger and better way the second time around. It is not over with him! These are challenges and setbacks wrought by the enemy, but Donald Trump is God's will for America, and God is a God of endless possibilities. This is why I'm not bothered, disturbed, or concerned in this moment, because long before the election I saw in a dream that Donald Trump is going to get back up and get back to work. Indeed it's not over until the Lord says so. Like so many others who heard the Lord say Donald Trump was His choice for reelection, I am waiting on the manifestation of God's purpose for our land and lives.

THE SIMPLE TRUTH

Some people insist that Donald Trump failed to handle the coronavirus pandemic well and that it was his failure to do so that led to his "defeat" in the November 3, 2020, election. But the plain truth is that if people had listened to him in the spring of 2020 when he said hydroxychloroquine works, America and the world would be a lot better off today. Thousands are using that medicine today and finding it incredibly effective in ridding them of their symptoms. If people had listened to the president when he publicly advocated the best treatment available, America wouldn't have lost as many lives to the virus as it has.

Indeed President Trump contracted the virus himself, and his recovery was swift. Unfortunately, a lot of doctors on the Left saw COVID as an opportunity to take President Trump out of the way, either through his own death or politically by blaming him for the devastation the virus caused. That was simply evil. It was also possibly greedy: doctors knew that COVID treatments were big money, costing much more than boring old hydroxychloroquine, which offers small profit margins by comparison. For example, remdesivir, a COVID medicine, costs $2,340 to $3,120 for a five-day course of treatment. It's IV-only and given in the hospital. That means business and money for the medical community.

Because politically motivated media kingpins and leaders mocked and misinformed people about hydroxychloroquine, the cost in lives and jobs was far more severe than it needed to be. As we witnessed and experienced, millions of people lost their jobs due to the shutdown of businesses, reduced job schedules, and loss of customers. In a study titled "A Statistical Analysis of Impact of COVID-19 on the Global Economy and Stock Index Returns," the authors wrote:

> The outbreak of pandemic COVID-19 across the world has completely disrupted the political, social, economic, religious, and financial structures of the world....More than 80 countries have closed their borders from transitioning countries, ordered businesses to close, instructed their populations to self-quarantine, and closed schools to an estimated 1.5 billion children. The world's top ten economies such as the United States, China, Japan, Germany, United Kingdom, France, India, Italy, Brazil, and Canada stand on the verge of complete collapse. In addition, stock markets around the world have been pounded, and tax revenue sources have fallen off a cliff. The epidemic due to infection is having a noticeable impact on global economic development.[2]

According to the International Labour Organization:

> New annual estimates confirm that labour markets around the world were disrupted in 2020 on a historically unprecedented scale. In 2020, 8.8 per cent of global working hours were lost relative to the fourth quarter of 2019, equivalent to 255 million full-time jobs. Working-hour losses were particularly high in Latin America and the Caribbean, Southern Europe and Southern Asia. Working-hour losses in 2020 were approximately four times greater than during the global financial crisis in 2009....Globally, the decline in working hours in 2020 translated into both employment losses and a reduction in working hours for those who remained employed, with significant variation across regions.[3]

A report by the *Guardian* forecasts that the monetary cost of the COVID pandemic "would total $28tn (£21.5tn) in lost output." That's twenty-eight trillion dollars!

Gita Gopinath, the IMF's economic counselor, described coronavirus as "the worst crisis since the Great Depression" and said "the pandemic would leave deep and enduring scars caused by job losses, weaker investment and children being deprived of education."

She added: "The cumulative loss in output relative to the pre-pandemic projected path is projected to grow from $11tn over 2020-21 to $28tn over 2020-25. This represents a severe setback to the improvement in average living standards across all country groups."[4]

A BBC report shows that "in the United States, the proportion of people out of work hit a yearly total of 8.9%, according to the International Monetary Fund (IMF), signaling an end to a decade of jobs expansion. Millions of workers have also been put on government-supported job retention schemes as parts of the economy, such as tourism and hospitality, have come to a near standstill. The numbers of new job opportunities is still very low in many countries. Job vacancies in Australia have returned to the same level of 2019, but they are lagging in France, Spain, the UK, and several other countries."[5]

Imagine if the world had embraced the relatively easy and available treatments for COVID-19 early on. Much of the financial and human toll could have been avoided.

MOVING FORWARD IN HEALTH

In many parts of the world, people are able to purchase hydroxy-chloroquine, ivermectin, and antibiotics over the counter. As part of my work, my staff and I continue to educate people that almost any of the quinoline medications work. These include hydroxychloroquine, nivaquine, chloroquine, or amo-diaquine. We encourage people all over the world, especially in places where malaria is endemic, to make sure they have their "Sunday-Sunday" medicine available, because it works both as a protective measure against COVID-19 and as effective early treatment if someone contracts the virus. I made a video about this on Rumble.com for people who want to see the step-by-step breakdown of what to do if they get sick.[6]

Drstellamd.com also offers COVID supplements, which are just enhanced-immunity vitamins including vitamin C, vitamin D, zinc, and quercetin. Quercetin is a zinc ionophore which, like hydroxychloroquine, opens zinc channels and allows zinc into the cells, helping to kill the virus.[7] People who cannot get hydroxychloroquine over the counter can order this supplement, and we can ship it to any part of the world.[8]

PRAY FOR DELIVERANCE, BUT PREPARE FOR TRIBULATION

As critical as it is to restore humanity's physical and political health, more important by far is our spiritual condition. Indeed Jesus promised that in days of great deception, wars and rumors of wars, the gospel of the kingdom will be preached to all nations for a witness. That points to nothing less than a global end-time revival. I believe that as we pray, God will hear us and come and rescue us with a great revival that reaches every neighborhood and home on the earth.

But we have to do our part. Every generation has to fight for its revival.

Every generation must contend for its generation.

Every generation must seek and find God for itself, or its faith would not be real.

In Noah's day, Noah preached righteousness. In fact, he was the only one preaching it! The rest of the world was corrupt and full of evil. Noah talked, but nobody listened, and God destroyed the world but saved Noah and his family.

Noah did his part—he preached, and he lived righteously.

In Sodom and Gomorrah lived a righteous man named Lot, whose soul was vexed by the sin that surrounded him. God called Abraham to intercede, and then God rescued Abraham's nephew, Lot, and his family before destroying Sodom and Gomorrah.

Abraham interceded. Lot remained righteous. They did their part in their generation.

In the days of Jezebel and Ahab, witchcraft was the official religion in Israel. The prophets were hiding in caves, afraid for their lives. God called a great prophet named Elijah, who set himself apart from that wicked society, walked in holiness before the Lord, and brought down fire from heaven. His brave stand caused revival to sweep through the land and restore prophecy and the fear of the Lord to its place of honor.

Elijah did his part in his generation.

The children of Israel were in Egypt, where God had said they would remain for 430 years. Then the cry of the people according to their bondage came up to God. God heard their cry and sent Moses to deliver them. Exodus 12:12 says God passed through the land of Egypt and executed judgment upon the gods of Egypt.

The people did their part and cried out to God in their generation. Moses too did his part to lead them.

All these accounts from the Bible instruct us that when

iniquity and evil rise to such high levels in society, the cry of righteous people reaches heaven. Even the cry of nature reaches God's ears. Then God calls forth preachers of righteousness like Noah, great men and women of faith like Abraham and Sarah, prophets like Elijah, and leaders like Moses to lead a willing generation out of captivity and into glorious victory.

THE CHURCH HAS THE POWER

God's first choice is never to destroy, but when iniquity and sin grow so thick in the land, judgment must come. The church is the only group of people on earth with the God-given ability to judge wickedness (see Psalm 149 for an example of what this looks like). Isaiah 53 says that no weapon formed against us will prosper, meaning we are protected as we go about God's righteous assignments in our day. I am telling you now, if the church will arise and fight the battle of our generation, praying and repenting before God and asking Him to intervene and judge wickedness, we can be saved. This is our calling right now on the earth.

Yet most people in the church don't want to judge wickedness. I make the funny statement that while God was taking the wheels off the chariots of Pharaoh to drown the riders in the Red Sea, today's Christians would have been putting the wheels back on and assuring Egypt not to worry, because God is love! These believers don't seem to understand their Bible, because it tells us many times that our God is also a man of war. If evil continues to grow, it has to be judged for good to be able to prevail. That duty is given to each believer. Jesus said His followers walk in the authority to "tread upon serpents and scorpions" (Luke 10:19). That isn't just about protecting ourselves from poison but calling us to destroy the destroyers!

If we decide we can "love everybody into the kingdom" and not judge anyone's behavior, we pridefully put our self-righteousness above God's true righteousness. Some Christians are so afraid of judging others that they almost want to love the devil himself with the love of the Lord! That is wickedness! The Bible says many times that we must hate wickedness, because God hates it. If we love wickedness, tolerate wickedness, and allow wickedness to infect the land, it's like walking into the house to see somebody raping your wife and harming your children, and you do nothing but love him with the love of the Lord. That is not proper; it's joining in wickedness.

The church must get into a warfare stance. We must start repenting. We must cry out to God to come down and release people from bondage and destroy the destroyers of humanity. There is no vacancy in creation. The prevailing priesthood in the land will rule the land. If the loudest noise is made by servants of the devil, they will rule the land. The church's noise—the united voice of prayer—must rise louder than the voice of sin and iniquity. That is why I and others are praying daily for revival in this nation. We have prayed hundreds of days already and are prepared to pray thousands more until God sends the answer in our generation.

That is our commitment to you, and to everyone living in our day. We will not fall down in our duty, because when God wants to redeem, save, or deliver, He calls His people to pray.

Prayer is not just begging God for an answer; it is exercising the spiritual authority we have been given. God gave the earth to the sons of men, and only when the sons of men speak will God act. Only when the sons of men do wickedness or ignore sin will the devil act. So if the sons of men do wickedness and fill the land with fornication, adultery, child molestation, and other garbage, it opens portals for demonic spirits to rule hearts and minds here. But when humanity starts serving and worshipping God and repenting, it opens portals for the Lord to come in power. Jesus said that if just two believers agree on some purpose of God, they will have the power to bind and release things in heavenly realms. In plain language, that means that whatever we allow on earth will happen on earth. Whatever we reject on earth will not happen. It is our choice.

The reason the world is going crazy is because the church has not taken her position to bind, loose, and decree and declare what will be and what will not be in our land. Jesus made it clear in Matthew 28 that our commission is to go into the world and disciple nations to God. This means teaching people the truth about God's kingdom and exposing the lies of the world's system.

When I drive around and pray, as I have done so many hours in my life, I don't just pray for myself or family alone; I pray for the people, that God will show them mercy. Nehemiah cried out on behalf of the wayward people in his generation, and Daniel repented on behalf of a sinful nation, though he himself was a righteous man. When we pray and repent on behalf of our nation and our children, we bind the spiritual powers of evil and loose the presence of God.

When I wonder whether or not God will answer, I recall a prophecy given more than a hundred years ago, in 1913. Maria Woodworth Etter, a powerful evangelist and revivalist in the United States, was concluding a revival and gave a prophecy in which she said: "We are not yet up to the fullness of the Former Rain and that when the Latter Rain comes, it will far exceed anything we have seen!"[9] That excites me! Similarly, William Seymour, of the Azusa Street Revival, in 1913 prophesied that a great revival would begin in one hundred years.[10] These are two of the many prophecies given about an end-time revival. Many prophets have prophesied the same thing about revival in our day.

When God speaks through His prophets, it is our responsibility to take those promises into battle and fight for them to come to pass. We fight in the prayer room, we contend for it in the sanctuary, we raise our voices in the city squares and on social media and in the hearing rooms and capitals of our nation. We call America back to being a city on the hill, a light to the world. Like Daniel and Joshua and Caleb and so many others, we rise up, cry out to God, and pull that prophecy out of the spirit realm and into the physical, where it can manifest as God intended it.

In the early church, when leaders in Jerusalem persecuted and jailed Christians, the Christian community didn't back off and try to "love" them into accepting Jesus. No! They went to praying that God would give them even more boldness, and as a result, the very building they prayed in shook as if from a violent earthquake. O God, let it happen again!

ALL CAN BE CLEANSED

When God's rain comes upon a land, it cleanses. It cleanses people of their sins and gives them a fresh start. It cleanses people of curses and generational bondage, like the people of God experienced in Egypt. I have prayed for people who grew up in witchcraft, dedicated to the devil, and God touched and redeemed them. Nothing is beyond the cross of Christ.

In our day people who took these experimental vaccines may feel they can't go back, that they compromised their genetic integrity. Some took the vaccine because they were scared. I have good news for you: the blood of Jesus is able to cleanse us from everything! He gave us the ultimate weapon against the enemy: our own repentance. God knows if you were scared. People who took these vaccines did not go out and fall into gross sin, even if the enemy is indeed at work to corrupt our "seed" through ever-more-clever and sinister means. Simply repent and let the blood of Jesus cleanse you. Pray for the fire of the Holy Ghost to come upon you. Pray until you sense in your spirit that there's been a cleansing and you can feel the presence of the Holy Spirit. He will heal you.

In our deliverance ministry, we often tell people to command strangers to come out of their body according to Psalm 18:43–45, which says,

> You have delivered me from the strivings of the people; you have made me the head of the nations; a people I have not known shall serve me. As soon as they hear of me they obey me; the foreigners submit to me. The foreigners fade away, and come frightened from their hideouts.

Foreign substances—including any foreign genetics in these vaccines—must submit to us, in Jesus' name. The same power of the Holy Spirit that raised the Lord Jesus from the dead is able to cleanse us. The Bible also says that even lawful captives shall be delivered. Isaiah 49:25 reads:

> But thus says the LORD: "Even the captives of the mighty shall be taken away, and the prey of the terrible be delivered; for I will contend with him who contends with you, and I will save your children."

So we pray and cry out for people to be pure in mind, body, and soul in a day when the world seeks to corrupt every part of our being in whatever way it can. But God will show mercy and cleanse us of all unrighteousness. I do believe that as revival sweeps through the land, whatever the enemy has done or accomplished in our bodies will be flushed out of people. Even if diabolical scientists and "dark artists" of modern sorcery succeed in polluting bloodlines of humanity, God has all power to cleanse those bloodlines and restore us. If God could redeem us as the seed of Adam, and make us a new creation, He can redeem anyone from any scheme of the enemy.

As I look back on these past two years, and the days going forward, I think back to my time in medical school and when I later met the Lord. I never in my wildest dreams thought I would be fighting for the soul of the world. But God called me and trained me in warfare and influence, as He has done with so many others. As a result of this grace, I have met so many wonderful people. At rallies and conferences they gather around and thank me and take pictures with me. People are so appreciative, telling me how my clinic or my efforts as a Frontline Doctor helped saved a family member. In all my years of medical practice, I never reached and helped so many people as I do now on a daily basis. As a doctor, I am thrilled by this!

Some people even embarrass me by calling me an American hero, but as I blush, this is music to my ears because I love this country. I never thought that a little girl from Cameroon would become one of America's doctors. The journey has almost been beyond words—and it has only just begun.

Now I pray that the presence of God will visit you and fill you and will visit this nation so that the glory of God fills the earth like the waters cover the sea. I pray that America and the nations of the earth will arise from the valley of dry bones and become a mighty army, taking back all the land lost to the clutches of the evil one. I pray and believe that our generation will rise higher than ever before and fight the battle God gives us, refusing to back down. With the courage of God saturating our hearts and the shouts of the Mighty One coming from our mouths, we will stand firm and take back the planet God gave us so He can once again fill it with His glory.

So Lord, we declare again—America will live!

PART II

I BELIEVE STRONGLY IN the power of teams and multiple voices rising up to speak and confirm the truth. For that reason, I asked friends and colleagues in the medical field to contribute individual articles relating to different aspects of what America is going through. These provide additional value and support to my message, and I believe God honors our coming together in unity around His purposes in our generation. Enjoy and be edified by these well-thought-out views and perspectives from people I admire and respect.

PART II

Chapter 10

HOW MASK WEARING DAMAGES MINDS AND HEARTS

By Avery M. Jackson, MD, Board-Certified Neurosurgeon

M Y INTEREST IN breathing freely began early, as I experienced asthma as a young boy. Competitive swimming helped ease my symptoms, and then in medical school at Wayne State University, I worked on aspects of respiratory function in a lab.

I added another branch to my professional pursuits and studied brain development, particularly in children. In my neurosurgery residency training at Penn State University, we had a combined pediatric and adult neurosurgery service. Instead of seeing pediatric patients for six months, which is typical exposure at most neurosurgery training residencies, we saw pediatric patients daily for five years. During that neurosurgery training, I received a peer-reviewed grant on shaken baby syndrome. We reviewed our experience focused on physiological and radiological confirmatory signs to this devastating form of abuse, which leads to brain damage and pulmonary compromise.

My knowledge of pediatric brain development and injury, as well as respiratory dysfunction, informs my views of what is happening today and the public "health" measures being demanded of people, especially children. In short, I am concerned.

First, as a practicing neurosurgeon for twenty years, having performed nine thousand surgical cases, I occasionally experience negative effects due to face mask wearing, even in very controlled environments. I feel better when breathing without the mask versus when I have it on. I experience a consistent difference in respiratory quality each time I don and doff the mask every day of my professional career. I have no desire to wear it any longer than I have to, even in the most controlled environment, the surgical operating suite.

Masks are not harmless, and their use should be considered judiciously. I can hardly imagine what our children experience while wearing masks during their critical years of intellectual, emotional, social, and physical brain development. To be honest, I initially didn't consider the effects of CO_2 retention from face mask wearing on children until my seven-year-old complained of headaches and began having problems focusing in school. A couple of articles come to mind to support my concern for unnecessary mask wearing, especially in our children. The first is titled "Effects of Carbon Dioxide on Brain Excitability and Electrolytes" by D. Woodbury et al., from the Department of Pharmacology at the University of Utah College of Medicine. They demonstrated:

> Effects of various concentrations of CO_2 on brain excitability and electrolyte distribution in rats were studied, and also some properties of seizures induced by abrupt withdrawal from high concentrations of CO_2.
>
> Inhalation of relatively low concentrations of CO_2 (5–20%) decreases brain excitability, as measured by an increase in electroshock seizure threshold (EST). In moderately high

concentrations (25–40%), CO_2 increases brain excitability, as measured by a decrease in EST and the appearance of spontaneous seizures. Inhalation of high concentration of CO_2 (40% or higher) markedly decreases brain excitability and causes anesthesia. Thus the effect of CO_2 on brain excitability is related to the concentration inhaled. Abrupt removal of rats from high (anesthetic) concentrations of CO_2 results in spontaneous clonic seizures within 30 seconds to 1 minute after withdrawal; these seizures last for 1–2 minutes. Inhalation of 50% CO_2 decreases brain intracellular Na and K concentrations and produces a marked cellular acidosis.[1]

A second article, in the January 2014 edition of *Biotechnic and Histochemistry,* titled "Effects of Carbon Dioxide Exposure on Early Brain Development in Rats," found that the developing brain is vulnerable to environmental factors. The researchers investigated the effects of air that contained 0.05, 0.1, and 0.3% CO_2 on the hippocampus, prefrontal cortex (PFC), and amygdala.

They "focused on the circuitry involved in the neurobiology of anxiety, spatial learning, memory, and on insulin-like growth factor-1 (IGF-1), which is known to play a role in early brain development in rats.

"Spatial learning and memory were impaired by exposure to 0.3% CO_2 air, while exposure to 0.1 and 0.3% CO_2 air elevated blood corticosterone levels, intensified anxiety behavior. In addition, apoptosis was increased, while cell numbers were decreased in the hippocampus and PFC after 0.3% CO_2 air exposure in adolescent rats. A positive correlation was found between the blood IGF-1 level and apoptosis in the PFC."

They "found that chronic exposure to 0.3% CO_2 air decreased IGF-1 levels in the serum, hippocampus and PFC, and increased oxidative stress. These findings were associated with increased anxiety behavior, and impaired memory and learning."[2]

In plain language, the animal studies demonstrated the negative effects of high CO_2 levels on the developing brain in rats and the negative effects after stopping the high CO_2 exposure.

Now consider CO_2's effect on humans. An article titled "The Influence of Carbon Dioxide on Brain Activity and Metabolism in Conscious Humans," published in the *Journal of Cerebral Blood Flow and Metabolism*, detailed efforts to gain "a better understanding of carbon dioxide (CO_2) effect on brain activity." This study investigates how an increase in blood CO_2 by inhaled CO_2 alters brain activity in humans, since findings in brain slices and anesthesia in animals provided evidence at the cellular level that higher CO_2 can have a profound effect on neural tissue.

This study used three techniques to assess the effect of CO_2 on brain activity. In their first study, they compared the participant's cerebral metabolism levels when breathing CO_2-enriched gases with breathing normal room-air gases.

In their second study, they investigated the spontaneous neural activity under normal CO_2 levels and high CO_2 levels by performing functional connectivity MRI (fcMRI).

In their third study, they looked at brain electrical activity via electroencephalogram (EEG) under room-air and CO_2 breathing conditions. A total of fifty healthy human subjects were used. These subjects were divided into four groups for different arms of the study:

1. The effect of CO_2 inhalation on cerebral metabolism

2. The cerebral metabolism control study

3. The effect of CO_2 on functional connectivity MRI

4. The effect of CO_2 on EEG

For the metabolism part, the experiment began with the subject breathing room air, establishing a normocapnic state, during which cerebral metabolism was determined. "The subject was then switched to the gas mixture containing 5% CO_2," and then they waited to allow for CO_2 rates to stabilize. The cerebral metabolism was measured again under stable conditions.

For the EEG part, the experiments were conducted for seventeen minutes. First they breathed room air, switched to the 5% CO_2 gas mixture, and then returned to room air. The EEG recordings were made continuously during this seventeen-minute period.

The results "first showed that hypercapnia reduced metabolic activity in the brain." Secondly, they showed that "CO_2 inhalation caused a decrease in spontaneous brain connectivity. Overall, [the] data showed a suppressive effect of CO_2 on brain activity."

This study "represents the first systematic investigation of this effect in conscious humans and suggests that resting-state neural activity is reduced due to mild hypercapnia. Further, [they] showed that this suppression of neural activity is accompanied by a reduction in metabolic [brain] activity."

These "findings suggest that increased CO_2 levels cause the brain to reduce metabolism and spontaneous neural activity, and enter a lower arousal state."[3]

All this scientific evidence confirms that prolonged exposure to CO_2 decreases brain activity and metabolism.

Think about it: your children and those with pulmonary or preexisting cerebral dysfunction, such as dementia and neurodegenerative disorders, brain injury, and so on, are emotionally and mentally impaired due to prolonged exposure to carbon dioxide. They are affected again when they transition to normal carbon dioxide levels after they take off their masks, with the potential to have disordered electrical brain activity manifesting as anything from poor overall brain function in absorbing schoolwork all the way up to seizures.

EMOTIONAL TOLL WITH FACE COVERINGS

Face coverings exact an emotional toll as well. Our heavenly Father told us to love Him and love one another. This requires the opportunity and ability to develop and maintain relationships. Relationship building is a greater challenge when you can't see a person's face. Even God shines His face upon us. When a face is covered, we don't know whether a person is smiling or frowning, happy or sad. Babies recognize facial expression early on, before verbal cues come into the picture.

Covering faces is like putting a prisoner into solitary confinement. It's a kind of emotional death sentence, a "solitary confinement" that can break even the hardest of criminal minds. God made us to have relationships. After He made Adam, He said that it is not good to be alone. Jesus inhabits our relationships.

There is evidence that mask mandates don't work in pandemics. Masks are not effective at blocking virus particles, like they are at blocking bacterial particles. The virus particles are too small. But masks do affect relationships and create fear and an unsettled population primed to make quick decisions regarding their health without coherently demanding solid data. Jesus said, "My sheep know my voice," and, "A voice of a stranger they shall not follow." (See John 10:27, 5.) Those who take God's Word literally hear, receive, believe, speak, and act on His Word. One develops a sensitive "ear" to hear the Holy Spirit's guiding. He is a gentleman. He doesn't force anyone. He guides and counsels. By spending time with the Holy Spirit, one becomes sensitive to His guidance.

Decisions are made from a perspective of fear or faith. When we are full of faith in God, we use our intellects to examine the choices for next steps on any given issue. We ask in faith with no wavering for the Holy Spirit to guide us to the correct choice. His peace fills us as He answers our questions. We then choose to do or not do something. It's a high-quality decision, not a reactive decision rooted in fear.

The Holy Spirit will always guide us into truth and reality. We can follow His peace and guidance, and we won't go wrong when we obey with a cheerful, obedient heart.

But these days, we need more people whose minds and emotions function in the beautiful, free way God designed them to. That means banishing physically and emotionally damaging "guidelines" and practices that do more harm than good, like mask wearing.

Chapter 11

LET AMERICA THINK

By Stefani Reinold, MD, MPH, Board-Certified Psychiatrist

YOU KNOW, YOU should probably tell your mom she can't come to visit next weekend," I told my husband, Travis, as he was relaxing in the living room.

"Why?" he asked.

"Because it's not safe!" I said somewhat adamantly.

My calm-in-the-storm, even-keeled, army veteran husband raised his eyebrows at me to suggest I was acting a bit unreasonable in the moment. It was a week after President Trump had issued his "fifteen days to slow the spread" guidelines, and like a typical law-abiding, pro–health care physician, I took these words with great care and caution. In hindsight I may have taken things a little too far. With my push to strictly order delivery food, keep my kids home at all costs, cancel trips to visit grandparents, and wipe down Amazon boxes, I was a far cry from my one-month-earlier self, who laughed in the face of danger and boldly faced the unknowns, a self who lived without fear. Within a short period of time I went from making spring break plans with my parents to being afraid to hug them for fear I would kill them.

"What happened? What changed?" I thought. "How did I seem to change overnight?"

Maybe you can relate. Maybe you wonder what happened to your mind or the minds of your friends, family members, colleagues, neighbors, clients, or faith leaders in recent days and years. Maybe you see the stark changes in yourself or your loved ones. And maybe you are working to return to normalcy—and find yourself oddly uncomfortable in that endeavor.

Whatever you think and however you feel, I've got you covered in this chapter. As a board-certified psychiatrist, mother of three young children, military wife, and believer in Christ, I want to share my personal story and professional perspective in hopes of educating, encouraging, and empowering you into the future. I will address how COVID-19 completely changed how we think—and how that happened. I will share how the pandemic hijacked neural wiring in our brains and discredited several psychological principles. Finally, I will illuminate the underground crisis throughout the COVID-19 pandemic: the mental health crisis.

THE MISSING ELEMENT

Instagram was my kryptonite—that is, until I was juggling a full-time private practice from home, homeschooling three children, running for school board, helping my husband, and managing a household. Bonus tip: if you need to free yourself from social media overconsumption, follow the tasks I mentioned.

In all seriousness, I love Instagram. Pretty photos, easy-to-consume content, good functionality—it has it all. But early in the pandemic I began to see the word *trauma* thrown around by Instagram influencers. This was not surprising to me, as I also agreed that the original shutdown would cause immense trauma for individuals. To be clear, I am talking about the first "fifteen days" and then the "thirty days" to slow the spread— not the hundreds of distressing things that happened after that in reaction to this pandemic. Even in those early weeks, many influencers and professionals alike gave lip service to *trauma*. But I never saw a clear explanation of what that means or any good guidance on what to do with it.

While many continue to talk about trauma, the conversation remains unfocused because frankly, we are still in a state of trauma.

What does trauma even mean? Trauma goes by many different definitions, depending on the individual or professional you talk to. I define *trauma* as follows: any experience that through its perception or lived experience creates a disruption to neural wiring that produces an over-activation of the sympathetic nervous system, often resulting in a common "fight, flight, or freeze" response.

Here are a few common questions:

Does everyone who experiences trauma develop post-traumatic stress disorder (PTSD)?

No. PTSD is a distinct clinical diagnosis where certain criteria are met, specifically including flashbacks (often in nightmares or reliving events), hypervigilance, and avoidance of trauma.

I haven't really had anything *that bad* happen to me. Can I still have trauma?

Yes. PTSD or PTSD symptoms don't depend on the severity of the trauma but rather on the perceived severity of the trauma and the individual's vulnerabilities to trauma or stress disorder symptoms.

I thought PTSD was only for combat veterans or sexual assault victims—is that true?

No. Symptoms of trauma can occur for a wide variety of significant life events, such as moving across country, being bullied in school, or getting fired from a job.

How do you prevent PTSD if you have had trauma?

There is no conclusive evidence suggesting that we have the power to prevent PTSD.[1] We do have certain lab markers, like cortisol levels in the blood, that may suggest whether an individual will go on to develop full-blown PTSD after a traumatic event.[2] Some experts have suggested that testimonial-style therapy, where individuals share their stories, may help to curb symptoms of PTSD.[3] At this time, there are no widespread, proven strategies to prevent PTSD, outside of preventing trauma in the first place.

FUNCTIONING WITH A TRAUMATIZED BRAIN

Back to Instagram. I know, I can't resist. While I was initially delighted to see trauma being discussed, I was disappointed that it likely fell on deaf ears, as many were just in "survival mode" for the first few weeks and months. I know I was. And when someone is actually *in* the state of trauma (i.e., survival mode), his or her brain is not in a place ripe for receiving and understanding information. Put another way, when you are in a state of trauma, you lose the capability to problem solve. Do you see why I started with this now?

Even in my private psychiatric practice outside Austin, Texas, I saw a significant drop in the number of patients receiving services in the months of late March, April, and May 2020. There are likely many reasons for this, but ultimately it is hard to talk about thoughts and feelings when you are in a state of shock, panic, and exhaustion.

Let me say this again. When you are in a state of trauma, you lose the ability to think critically. How does this happen? Well, you have a special part of your brain called the amygdala that is directly responsible for sensing threats and driving fear in your brain. Interestingly, we know from solid research that individuals with anxiety often have a highly advanced amygdala because much of anxiety is driven by fear.[4] The amygdala has an important function to keep us safe and, specifically for mothers, to keep our children safe. However, if left to its own devices, the amygdala is not a good master. This, I think, is why it is not situated in the front of our brain, a subtle signal to us that it should not be the leader but a conscious bystander.

When the pandemic shutdown first happened in March 2020, many of us became obsessed with the media. Frankly, most of what we were hearing only stoked our fear and did little to comfort or console us. Media does this by design. They call it entertainment, but it's really an assault on our amygdala, inciting fear and emotion to drown out critical thinking. It is no wonder then that so many of us (myself included) were easily persuaded by information we were receiving, even if that information was of inconsistent scientific veracity. Isn't this the argument we've had all year? We call each other sheep, and we don't understand how our friends blindly follow any and all information being given to them, even if the source of the information has long been discredited.

The answer is simple: trauma. The original shutdown was

traumatic. And the ensuing effects of the following year (2021) continued to be traumatic. It is traumatic to face financial crisis, to fear for your own health and safety, to lose loved ones, to go through divorce, to not see your family for extended periods of time, to see your life as you know it completely change overnight. Heck, it's traumatic to homeschool your kids and be home with your husband all day. OK, maybe that's going too far, but you get the point.

If you can understand that every single individual is living in a collective state of trauma (albeit some significantly worse than others), it will help you immensely to hold compassion for people. Again, trauma prevents you from being able to activate your frontal lobe, where executive functioning, problem solving, and planning reside. And trauma keeps you in a perpetual "fight, flight, or freeze" place. Next time the lady in the store goes off on you for not wearing a mask, take a deep breath and remember that she's doing the best she can too.

UNDERGROUND PANDEMIC

If you are uncomfortable with the word *trauma*, let's first agree that 2020 was a stressful year. Stress is a word we throw around so much that it can be hard to assign meaning or depth to it. To help, let me share a tool we use called the Holmes-Rahe Stress Inventory. This inventory helps us quantify certain life experiences to predict a stress-related health breakdown.

According to the scale, different life events, both positive and negative, are given a score. For example, death of a spouse is scored at 100, marriage is scored at 50, moving is scored at 20, and vacation is scored at 13. Major personal illness is scored at 53. The sum directs us to a level of risk for health complications. A total score greater than 150 is associated with significant risk of health breakdown within two years' time.[5]

Furthermore, we know that economic stability has direct correlation to health problems as well, specifically mental health. Every percentage point increase in unemployment leads to higher mortality rates.[6] This is largely why, prior to 2019, many studies recommended keeping social life as normal as possible in any response to a pandemic. It seems as though no COVID task force in the country bothered to familiarize themselves with this information.

Outside of advocating for early treatment for COVID (something Dr. Immanuel talks at length about), protecting the social and economic stability of the country would have surely saved lives. Now I fear we are on a high-speed train in the wrong direction. Our country is more economically unstable than in years past, and with that has come unnecessary harms, specifically mental health harms.

Mental health issues skyrocketed in 2020. Every single metric that we look at, from new onset of symptoms to hospitalizations to suicides, increased throughout the pandemic. Substance abuse and eating disorders are on the rise. Self-injurious behaviors and suicides have increased. Domestic violence in families has been prevalent.[7] The suffering is exacerbated by the fact that there is a provider shortage. Psychiatric patients wait weeks or months to see a provider in the outpatient setting.[8] These same patients wait in emergency rooms days to sometimes weeks to find a bed in an inpatient psychiatric facility.[9] Furthermore, mental health providers themselves are burned out and emotionally exhausted from the ravages of 2020. The mental health crisis was not created solely from the pandemic, but the response to the pandemic has driven a grave situation that will take years to recover from.

MASKS AND MENTAL HEALTH

Now let's turn to a subject I hate: masks.

Despite my initial preoccupation with sanitizing my home and abiding by all of Sir Fauci's commands, I never liked masks. Throughout medical school and in my master's in public health program, I never once was told that masks prevent viral transmission. I never once heard that masks did anything to help stop the spread of infectious diseases. I never read a single study before 2019 that demonstrated anything but that face masks are ineffective at decreasing viral transmission. Even in the beginning of the COVID-19 pandemic, Anthony Fauci himself instructed individuals not to wear a face mask. Several states even have anti-mask laws. Still, mask mandates came in full force across the country and were touted as an instrumental component of decreasing the spread of disease, even though this has not definitely been proved true. Studies before 2020 concerning the use of face masks have shown their inability to significantly affect the risk of viral transmission. In my opinion, the only reason so many agreed was because of the state of trauma we were all in. Remember the inability to think critically?

I know I am preaching to the choir here, but I would like to share my perspective as a psychiatrist. Not only do masks affect the ability to speak, hear people, read body language, and develop proper phonics and language development; they also impede the ability to convey facial expressions, which drive subconscious and conscious communication of empathy. With covered faces, we have a difficult time receiving and giving validation, assurance, encouragement, and sympathy. Ironically, these are the built-in forms of comfort that we so desperately craved during the first year of the pandemic. Masks impede the ability to express the deepest and greatest level of humanity. On top of a lack of physical touch (which also expresses empathy) and physical separation from community, we literally lose the ability to be comforted. When I imagine the harm that this level of social isolation causes, I think of two specific psychology experiments.

One is facial-feedback hypothesis, which says that one's facial expressions directly affect one's emotional experience. It counters the assumed belief that "we smile because we are happy" with the alternative "we are happy because we smile." Meaning, it is the facial expressions on their own that help to cause different emotional states in our body.

To illustrate this in real time, smile right now. Keep smiling. I know it feels awkward, but how do you feel? Do you notice even a small inkling of joy bubbling up? Now make a frown. Unless you are a small toddler, this is actually a very difficult facial expression to make for most people. Frowning requires the use of far more facial muscles than smiling does. But keep frowning as best you can. How do you feel? Do you still feel happy? Or do you notice yourself getting irritated, a little agitated, sad, or angry? If you do not feel these effects, practice holding these facial expressions slightly longer. I promise, you will feel the effects.

Now think back to the last time you wore a mask. Did you smile more or less? Did you make eye contact more or less? Were you able to make proper facial expressions in conversations with other people? My guess is that you are much like me in that even the sheer wearing of a mask restricts your ability to make facial expressions properly. Depending on how long one wears a mask in a day, this can have severe effects on daily living and provoke significant mental health issues.

The still-face experiment, conducted by developmental psychologist Edward Tronick in the 1970s, showed that when mothers looked at their babies with a "still face"—a face that was void of facial expressions—the babies became deeply uncomfortable, agitated, hopeless, and withdrawn.[10] You can search "Still Face Experiment" online to watch the videos for yourself. This research has propagated theories on how postpartum depression can affect the mental health and development of infants.[11]

Now consider that the vast majority of daycares around the world have teachers who are masked all day trying to nurture and care for infants and toddlers. If Tronick's research showed distress in as little as a few seconds, what do you think an entire day is doing? I can speak from my own experience with my baby in childcare in 2020. She was in daycare with teachers who wore masks all day from the time she was seven months until eleven months before I pulled her out for these exact concerns. In those brief months, my baby barely took naps at daycare. Normally, infants nap several hours during the day. Every day when I picked her up from daycare, she was stressed and on the verge of tears. And, mind you, this is my third baby, so I'm aware of what a normal level of exhaustion is at the end of a day away from mom. This was different. Sadly, even as an expert, I did not see these signs until I pieced it all together several months later when I finally brought her home. Once at home, she began sleeping appropriately again and has shown no signs of stress that I previously saw.

Emotional stress is not so obvious to us. It's why we as a

society overlook mental health issues in general, and specifically during the first year of the pandemic. We all have suffered some form of emotional struggle, some worse than others. When we ignore or avoid stressors in our daily lives, it will always come out in emotional health suffering. One such example is found in the stark rise in a previously rare symptom in the mental health field: derealization.[12]

Derealization is the feeling that the reality around you is altered or not real. I almost chuckle when I write that sentence because, *duh*! Yes, the world around us is altered. Yet, in all of my patients who have struggled with derealization during the pandemic, none of them knew why they were experiencing it. Derealization is frequently a symptom that happens after significant trauma and is usually associated with PTSD symptoms. While some patients did exhibit other symptoms consistent with PTSD, many of my patients had derealization without any other symptoms at all. This is often very difficult to treat as it requires addressing the underlying trauma that led to this experience in the first place.

To help my patients, I have to point out the significant trauma of their current life. Interestingly, many patients deny that their lives are "that bad." They erroneously assume that because they have not experienced significant loss, obvious hardship, or change in their daily lives, they have not experienced trauma. While I commend their desire for resilience, I fear it is this exact emotional resilience that continues to exacerbate the derealization. They are consciously seeing their lives as normal when unconsciously their minds understand this world is anything but normal. Many aspects of our livelihoods have been completely altered, and while some have experienced worse effects than others, all of our worlds have changed. The difficulty in accepting this stems from a concept I call the Prosperity Fallacy.

THE PROSPERITY FALLACY

By the fall of 2020, I was seeing an explosion of need and numbers in my outpatient psychiatric private practice. It was overwhelming to witness so much suffering in school-aged children. I saw symptoms I was not used to seeing, like derealization, and was witnessing more pronounced symptoms in otherwise emotionally well individuals. Frankly, I did not always have a solution to their problems. Medications and therapy tools that had worked wonders in the past were not making a dent in treatment. In fact, many patients continued to deteriorate right before my eyes. And this was in Texas, a state that was operating more normally than many other states. Our schools were not shut down for lengthy periods of time. Most businesses were open. Many people were back to work in some capacity. The economy was stable. But I knew this wasn't normal. And my patients did too.

I worried specifically that this new reality we had created was causing harm. Of course, through my lens as a psychiatrist, I think it was causing more harm than potential benefit. So I began to speak out. I shared thoughts on my social media. I talked to parents, friends, and neighbors. Some listened, some brushed me off, and others thought I was outright crazy. I began advocating to my local school board, sharing my concerns that school-related COVID protocols were causing more harm than benefit and would lead to long-term mental health consequences in children and teens. Even after countless emails and speeches at local meetings, nothing changed. I felt like no one heard me. No one cared.

The challenge I kept receiving was something I now describe as the Prosperity Fallacy. It was the refrain of "I'm just happy my kids are in school" or "I'm just happy I have a job" or "I'm just happy I have a great home." While I appreciate a focus on the positive, I was disappointed to hear the constant "good is good enough" message. To me, this was not good. This was a downright scary parallel universe that everyone was living in and pretending was OK. This was a world where we were beginning to normalize child abuse. Yes, masks on children for seven-plus hours a day is child abuse. This was not good at all. What happened? How did we get here?

Well, remember the whole trauma thing? When trauma becomes more consistent and chronic, we become conditioned to a new level of personal values and expectations. We get conditioned to a "new normal." Imagine a wife who has suffered abuse at the hands of her husband. She once loved this man. Maybe she has children with this man. She is confused at first by the abuse. "Why?" she asks herself. She loves him and wants what she thinks is best for her children, so she stays with him despite the abuse. Or maybe she truly has no other options for residence or financial resources. So she endures the abuse. Time and again this happens. It takes an average of seven times for someone to leave an abusive loved one.[13] Many more don't even attempt to escape but live in abuse indefinitely.

Why do we stay in a place of trauma? Why would we actively stay in a place where we are being mistreated? Why would a woman stay with an abusive spouse? Two reasons. First is that her fear of the alternative (living alone with no shelter, no money, no food, etc.) overpowers the fear of the status quo (living in the abuse). Second is that due to chronic trauma, her brain has adapted a response known as "learned helplessness."[14]

Can we see similarities between the abused wife and the state of our country at large? Again, this is why I began this chapter through the lens of trauma. Without an understanding of trauma, we cannot begin to understand the psychological ramifications of the pandemic.

In a place of trauma that began with the initial lockdowns of March 2020, many individuals were overpowered by a fear of the virus, then with a fear of daily living. Because of the censoring of information about early treatment, the liberal counting of COVID deaths, and endless communication about the pandemic on television and social media, we were programmed to feel bad, selfish, or even amoral if we challenged anything related to protecting the well-being of others. Instead of sharing a matter-of-fact view of the function of the virus, evidence-based prevention strategies, and early treatment protocols, we got never-ending, fear-driven media messages with seemingly one mission: to make us comply. And so many became like the frog slowly boiling in water and not realizing where it was leading.

Interestingly enough, there was a stronger fight for freedom in states and countries where lockdowns were the worst, because I think those residents saw more obviously the harm being done. In states such as Texas that were operating relatively well, individuals adopted this "we should just be happy" mindset: the prosperity fallacy. Just because you are not homeless, filing bankruptcy, ending your marriage, or losing a loved one to COVID does not mean you are not suffering. Remember my definition of *trauma* from earlier: it is not defined by the severity of the event but by the subjective neurological interpretation of the event. Trauma has affected all of us, even those of us living in prosperity.

SOCIAL DESPAIR

Nowhere has trauma affected us more than in our elderly and nursing homes. I have a sweet patient I will call Judy. Judy is seventy-eight years old and was diagnosed with Parkinson's disease a few years ago. She came to see me shortly after her diagnosis, as she was experiencing significant depression—a biological phenomenon common in many Parkinson's patients as dopamine diminishes in their brains. In the year prior to the pandemic, she improved significantly in both her motor symptoms from Parkinson's as well as her mood symptoms from depression. She had gotten to a place where she was living almost independently again. This was a wonderful thing for her, as her biggest stressor was being a burden on her loved ones.

Then COVID happened.

Judy went from being a stable, joyful, improving patient to a complete shell of her former self. She was forced to stay in her nursing home and could not see peers, could not see family, could not eat meals in the cafeteria, and could not even get her hair cut. A woman from an era where social media and technology did not rule her childhood, she was now forced to live most of her life online—a difficult medium for some, and impossible for her. She was miserable.

As a psychiatrist, I am trained well to hold strong boundaries of emotions. I often hear horrific stories from my patients, and in order to best hold hope and space for healing, I must keep strong in those sessions. I show proper expressiveness but try to contain myself in situations where my emotions may cause further suffering for the patient. With Judy, it was hard. How could I pretend like everything was normal when she felt locked up in a cage like an animal? These were her actual words to me in one particularly emotional session. How could I tell her everything would get better when I was not sure it would?

At one point in 2020, I thought I might lose Judy. I received a call from one of her daughters. She informed me that Judy had stopped eating. Her daughter was not allowed to enter the nursing home to talk to her, and Judy had stopped answering her FaceTime calls. Her daughter continued to bring her care packages and letters from her grandkids, but she felt helpless. She was reaching out to me to fix the problem. We doctors do not like to admit that we cannot fix a problem. We want to solve everyone's problems. We want to heal people. We want to save people. That is what we were trained to do. Being in a place of helplessness myself was a horrible feeling to endure.

In a moment of my own helplessness as a doctor, I simply prayed.

> *Dear Lord, thank You for the blessing to be able to help those in need. Right now I am helpless. I can't do anything to help. Please save Judy. Give her the will to eat. Revive her soul to live. Grant her life again. Her life is not over yet. In Jesus' name, amen.*

This was not the first time that prayer felt like my only battle tool, and it will not be the last. While I can share that Judy is still alive and well, I cannot say the same for everyone in similar circumstances. Our elderly have faced a terrible battle in the pandemic. Beginning with the horrors of nursing home deaths in New York City, effects from the virus, and the ongoing social isolation and emotional ramifications, our elderly have suffered greatly.

While we in America frequently see our minds and bodies as two distinct entities, this is not accurate. Our minds and bodies are intricately intertwined. How we feel emotionally affects our physical health, and often our physical health affects how we feel emotionally. Many experts go so far as to say that our emotional health drives every aspect of our physical health. Nothing drives our emotional health more than social connection to others.

One of the earliest, and most chronic, driving factors of emotional distress was the social isolation. Y'all may know this as "social distancing." I am sorry, but I call BS on that. Where did the "six feet" metric come from anyway? Social distancing was a fancy term coined to give credence to something that we otherwise would have considered sheer torture. Children were not able to play with friends at recess or sit next to peers in the cafeteria or in classrooms. Elderly people were not allowed to leave their nursing home rooms. Family members and friends were not allowed to see one another for social events and holiday gatherings. Customers must stand on silly dots on the floor at grocery stores and limit how many people they can eat with at a table at a restaurant.

My constant question is: What are the mental health ramifications of this? If we understand that our emotional health is not only important but also has life-or-death consequences, then we must always consider the risks of mental health repercussions. That was never discussed. In many of the initial COVID task forces, from the White House to states to local school districts, there were no mental health professionals weighing in. Given the recommendations that were given, this is no surprise. Yet sadly, we have paid a price for that.

DISCOMFORT WITH NORMAL

At the time of this writing, I work a job out of state, far from home. While Texas ventures back to mostly normal, other states and countries around the world are pushing further lockdowns and further infringement of personal liberties. In the hospital I currently work in, I noticed a new policy: no masks indoors for those who have been fully vaccinated. This comes after the overlords of the CDC announced this same recommendation.[15] Yet what I find most interesting is that I have yet to see a single hospital employee dare to remove his or her face covering. It is not because they are not vaccinated. They all have their vaccination status tagged prominently on their hospital ID badges—"COVID Vaccinated" next to a cute, attention-getting graphic. Still, no one removes their masks.

I always assumed that people were waiting for express permission from some source of authority—government officials, teachers, pastors, parents, business owners—in order to take off their masks and live a free and normal American life. And yet time and time again I have seen that even when government regulations have been lifted, individuals continue to wear masks. Even when there is no law or punishable offense, people are afraid of returning to normal.

We cannot understand this phenomenon without understanding the traumatic nature of 2020. Indeed, it all comes back to trauma. How individuals respond to trauma is unique to their specific life experiences. Some individuals will "fight" in a state of trauma, meaning they will rebel, push limits, or challenge circumstances. Some individuals will "flee" in a state of trauma, meaning they will want to avoid the experience at all costs. And some individuals will "freeze" in a state of trauma, meaning they will have a hard time making any meaningful progress in their behaviors and actions.

Regardless of how someone responds individually to trauma, we can agree that 2020 demonstrated a textbook example of social conditioning. Social conditioning is defined as the sociological process of training individuals in a society to respond in a manner approved by the society in general and peer groups within society. And the minute society changed rhetoric from protecting ourselves to protecting others was the minute we began to dismantle individual choice over their health.

While it is a noble concept to want to care for our fellow brethren, it is a slippery slope in public health, as it now creates a subconscious moral hierarchy whereby "pro-maskers" are moral and "anti-maskers" are amoral. And this is why it is so hard for some people to return to normal. From 2020 onward, they have been conditioned to believe that to be a good person, they must follow several different protocols, including wearing a mask. They came to believe that if they did not do these things, they must be horrible human beings who want to kill people. It is no wonder they now have a hard time changing course.

Social conditioning mixed with a state of trauma is a dangerous combination leading to something I referenced earlier: learned helplessness. Learned helplessness is "behavior exhibited by a subject after enduring repeated aversive stimuli beyond their control."[16] You do not even want to know the cruelty toward animals inflicted in research studies in order to prove this concept. I will just tell you it involved dogs and fences and electrical zaps.[17] But learned helplessness is widely accepted to explain how many individuals with a history of trauma behave. Again, you may still have a hard time accepting the fact that 2020 was traumatic, but indeed it was.

The never-ending news stories of death, the constant threat of death, the fear of losing your job or business, the chaos around childcare while working from home, and the isolation from friends and family are just some of the many examples of trauma perpetuated throughout the pandemic. Not to mention the overt censorship of preventive and early treatment options for the virus which caused ongoing existential fear and helplessness in so many individuals.

This is why business owners, school districts, university campuses, athletic organizations, and even government officials have a difficult time making decisions right now. We have all been trained to wait on and follow recommendations from higher-ups. This also explains why for a significant majority of 2020, most states and locales looked very similar. It is only now, at the time of this writing, that we have started to see different courses of action ruling the future and true colors being revealed.

In medicine, "the cure cannot be worse than the disease." Many people somehow forgot this wisdom in 2020. Any treatment we recommend in medicine ought to be driven by a risk assessment that considers all harms, benefits, and common side effects.

If you are still feeling a discomfort to return to normal, that is OK. Trauma affects us all differently. I encourage you to continue to challenge why you feel the way you do, acknowledge what led to these thoughts and feelings, and inquire what limiting beliefs may still be holding you back. We can responsibly return to normal. The faster we do, the less further suffering we will endure.

I must properly acknowledge the bountiful blessings bestowed upon me by my Lord and Savior, Jesus Christ. All that I accomplish is through the power of the Holy Spirit and God's endless grace in my life. I am blessed beyond measure with the best husband, encouraging family, healthy children, and respectful colleagues.

Dr. Immanuel tells us often that this pandemic was/is a spiritual battle. I agree. While I strongly encourage anyone who is suffering physically and emotionally to reach out for help, know that healing your physical self is only one step of a much deeper journey. I invite you to take that journey toward "big T" Truth.

As you do, keep freeing yourself from fear, folly, and false-hoods. Live free, think for yourself—and don't be afraid to visit your in-laws.

Chapter 12

A PEDIATRICIAN'S VIEW: KIDS, COVID-19, AND A DIVINE HAND

By Angelina Farella, MD, Pediatric Medical Director

for America's Frontline Doctors

IT WAS DECEMBER 2019, and I was getting ready for just another day—the morning chaos of kids eating breakfast, scurrying around gathering school books, settling in for the homeschool day. I was just about to shut off the TV when I heard the local news story: forty-four reported cases of a SARS-like virus in China.[1] I turned to my husband and said, "Something's up. Why would they report on forty-four people in a country of more than one billion?" I was suspicious, and my gut instinct was that I needed to remain vigilant.

About a month later I was on a plane to Los Angeles on my way to a conference, my first flight in many years, when I saw a news report of an airplane from China being quarantined in the same airport I had just landed in.[2] I am always aware that we Americans are just one plane ride away from potential disaster. I thought, "Really! Good gracious, I don't want to be the one who brings this back to Houston!" My one-plane-ride-away theory was coming to fruition.

Shortly after that, the United States began restricting non-US residents coming in from China. Death tolls were mounting in a place called Wuhan, China. We learned it was a SARS-like coronavirus named SARS-CoV-2, or COVID-19. Lockdowns started in China and spread throughout Europe and other areas.

I use my Facebook page for "Doc in the Box" and "Walk With a Doc" live videos on topics that help parents with their kids. Typically I discuss things such as tips for picky eaters, gut health, and hydration. Now I coached my asthmatic patients to increase their vitamin D intake and start their preventive medications such as budesonide, to not run low or out of their asthma medications, and to take vitamin supplements. Once the pandemic was in full swing, my topics changed to tips on mental health and how to boost the immune system and protect against viruses, suggesting vitamin D, probiotics, antioxidants such as CoQ_{10}, getting exercise outside, sunshine therapy, handwashing, taking over-the-counter medications such as cimetidine (Tagamet), and using tonic water because it had quinine in it—nothing too technical, nothing too fancy. I was even initially on board with "flattening the curve," an exercise estimated to last about two weeks, since the infectivity period was thought to be up to fourteen days. The resemblance to the varicella (chicken pox) virus came to mind, where infectivity is ten to twenty-one days from exposure. It made sense to me at the time. I thought we could really slow the spread if we all waited the two weeks.

Well, so much for that! The lockdowns dragged on and on.

Case numbers continued to climb, and it became apparent that this virus was going to act like a really bad influenza season. My thoughts were, "Let's go back to normal then and treat those that are sick." Then things just got weird. Local news advised sick people to stay home. I was astounded and appalled at the same time. On my Facebook Live videos I spoke about shutting off the news because of the rampant misinformation and fearmongering that was causing anxiety to skyrocket. WHO had declared a pandemic, and patients were being told not to see their doctors if they were sick? What was worse, hospitals were shutting down elective, diagnostic, and preventive procedures. Hospitalization rates were rising, and the news reports sounded as if there were an apocalypse in the ICUs. Most of my appointments became virtual due to patient fear of coming to the office because the evening news told people it was a great place to get infected with COVID. Ugh! I racked my brain to remember any incidence of a patient catching an illness in my office.

Besides, the kids weren't a factor in the numbers. Most were not getting sick, even if their parents were.[3] I read any early-outcome studies I could find from China and was surprised yet pleased to see children were not severely affected.[4] In fact, they were less likely to be infected even if exposed to an actively ill adult in the household.[5] They were actually buffers to adults! This was a relief. I knew this to be true here in my community because parents were calling me to help them or their adult family members who couldn't find a doctor to treat them. The media pushed people to stay home and not go to the doctor but wait until they got sicker to go to the ER. I was getting frustrated with the hogwash the American people were being fed. The death toll was rising, and it seemed to me it was because of the TV news. I was increasingly upset hearing stories about patients going to the ER, being given acetaminophen (Tylenol), and then being sent home with no treatment. I could not believe it. No treatment for a respiratory virus? I knew that bronchodilators and inhaled corticosteroids via nebulizers were very helpful in respiratory diseases.

Then I heard one of the most ridiculous things ever: nebulizers were taken off the ambulances and out of patient treatment areas! Immediately I called my durable medical equipment company and told them to stock me up with nebulizers.

The death toll ticker displayed on the news wasn't going to deter me. I wasn't going down without a fight. I became a doctor to help people. Doctors' offices were closing their doors. I thought, "Isn't this what we signed up for? Isn't this our duty, to treat the sick to the best of our ability?" Doctors were going bankrupt in a pandemic![6] An ultimate irony. Telemedicine went crazy, as if laying hands on a patient was not necessary. Children need to get their well checks, vaccinations, and therapies.

Our office remained open to our patients, but no one came for weeks.

REDISCOVERING HYDROXYCHLOROQUINE

I searched as much as I could for a treatment that maybe none of us really knew about. My rabbit hole research of old SARS, MERS, and Ebola studies on therapeutics led me to hydroxychloroquine, remdesivir, and some medications studied in the HIV studies. Of these, hydroxychloroquine seemed the most likely to be available in the outpatient setting to my patients since it was safe in children and pregnant women. I figured that in a pinch I could at least try the influenza antivirals since coronavirus was also an mRNA virus. I had prescribed hydroxychloroquine/chloroquine for years to my mission families going to endemic malaria areas in the past. I have always been a big cheerleader for nutraceuticals and carry some in the office. I was glad to see that vitamins D and C and zinc were part of the treatment, so I made sure I was stocked up with vitamins, probiotics, rehydration solution, and antioxidants for my patients' families. I did another Facebook Live about treatment and prevention—and got two thousand views![7] This was far more than the two hundred or so I would get before this for other topics. People were looking for answers.

I saw another news report showing the world map that overlapped areas endemic for malaria and the areas where COVID was causing significant hospitalizations and mortality. Could it be coincidental that the endemic malaria countries had low COVID numbers? Could it be that the need to use hydroxychloroquine to prevent malaria also protected the population from COVID?

I started thinking back to the Flunami of the 2017–2018 season. At that time, the flu hit the United States, and I was seeing sixty or more patients daily for nearly a week. The press didn't mention it being a pandemic and didn't keep a ticker of positive cases. The United States attributed approximately eighty thousand deaths to the flu that season.[8] Doctors did not close their offices. I bet they stayed open after their closing hours to help those who beckoned. I know we did. The hospitals were busy and ICUs filled up, but there was no public panic that care and treatment would not happen. There was no call for extra personal protective equipment or the wearing of masks. We did what needed to be done: covered our coughs and sneezes, washed our hands, took extra vitamins, and if inclined got a flu shot.

But the news now was all gloom and doom. Schools and businesses were closed down. Only if you were "essential" were you able to remain open. Shortages of food, toilet paper, and personal protective equipment for frontline workers was all the focus. I noted inconsistencies in the reporting, such as "positive cases" versus "symptomatic patients." Hospitalization numbers, especially the ICU bed counts, were strangely exaggerated. I proved this with our own local hospital system reports.[9] I got on Facebook and did a live video ("Doc in the Box #27, #31") to show folks where to find the real numbers and how to understand the graphs on inpatient numbers. My viewership went to 137,000 with hundreds of comments and 2,000 shares![10] This was a total shock to me. I had no idea what "going viral" even meant. Apparently people were either really bored or looking for answers. I believe it was the second.

Now parents of kids were asking about school. "Doc in the Box #29" presented the pros and cons of sending kids to school, using logic and reason. I made a wave with twelve thousand views.[11] I got attacked, though. There were people just losing it over the kids "[bringing] COVID home" to elderly family members, and how could I be so cavalier about letting them return? I approached this subject by teaching people how to make a pro/con list so they could make the best decision for their families. Some people just prefer not to listen but rather to assume and attack. I let it roll off my back.

A WORLD GONE MAD

It was July 2020, and school was still up in the air. COVID in kids had a very low incidence since the beginning of the pandemic. In fact, as of July 31, 2020, seventeen states had reported no deaths under age eighteen.[12] But what about the flu? Well, kids and the flu are two peas in a pod. They can spread influenza more efficiently than bees making honey.

Why? Hygiene, for one. They do not observe personal space, so they pick it up and share it with everyone else. Entire classrooms go down during flu season. This is what I worried about when SARS-CoV-2 started. Kids generally are the vectors of most infectious diseases. Between January 16 and February 8, 2020, around 2,135 pediatric patients were studied. More than 90 percent of all patients were asymptomatic, with mild or moderate cases. Infants were more likely to have more-severe disease (about 10 percent of all severe cases), and all contracted it from household contacts.[13] I shared this information in the "Doc in the Box" videos, but to some it did not matter.

The divide between what physicians were saying among themselves and the narrative of the mainstream media became increasingly noticeable to me. On social media there were pictures of patients wearing masks with subtitles like "Isn't this cute?" Frankly, the pictures of children wearing masks holding teddy bears or dolls wearing masks were appalling to me. The pictures of their dolls in masks matching with their young caretakers kept reminding me of doing rounds on the oncology (cancer) floor, where the kids wore masks to protect themselves from others. Those kids were going through chemotherapy and other treatments that really knocked out their immune systems. In contrast, now I was looking at pictures of healthy children wearing colorful cloth masks of all different kinds, sometimes matching their parent or teddy bear or doll. This was gut-wrenching! I had to pull myself off these sites. I couldn't even think about commenting on how grotesque this was to me, noting the comments from other physicians that were also explaining how cute and wonderful and protective these things were for their small-patient population.

It was at this point that I started to realize medicine may

be all but lost. This wasn't just a differing opinion; this was an outright lie being accepted by scientifically trained professionals, those in charge of the health and advocacy of children. I've long regarded myself as an advocate for children. I treat each one of my patients as if he or she were my own. My patients know that because I have repeated this mantra often in the office when we have dealt with difficult situations. The families I have grown to know and love over the years have always understood that we are a team, in this fight together. I truly believe there are many doctors just like me out there.

But what was going on in the summer of 2020 made me start to think I was one in a million, a rarity, an outlier, a turtle on a post. I decided to become an independent thinker, and I started looking for those like me. I knew there had to be some people out there, so I initiated an exhaustive search. I recalled having seen videos of some physicians who were speaking out about certain treatment modalities. I decided to contact those doctors. I understood why they didn't return my calls. They didn't know their friends from their enemies. I contacted on social media another doctor whose video I watched and agreed with. I asked him to call me at his earliest convenience. Initially his call back shocked me. I did not view this person as a peer but as a hero! I was so enthralled that he took the time to give me a call and share with me his treatment plan so I could help in this fight too.

He told me his experience with other doctors across the country and asked me to try to recruit others like us. He sent me the main protocol that they knew was working and shared with me his results on treating his patients. All of this data was registered very quickly in my brain. I viewed this man as a fighter, a warrior, and someone willing to do what was right to help his patients. I was so elated to find there were other doctors like me who felt doing nothing was doing harm.

Now I was equipped—now I was ready! He knew I had virtual-visit capability, and since his office was five hours away, any overflow he could not help he sent to me. Our doors were open virtually for those seeking treatment—and there was no shortage of those seeking treatment. The patients' gratitude was overwhelming. Many of them feared they would not survive this outbreak. Once a few patients received successful acute treatment, word spread quickly. We set up a tent outside the office to examine and do IVs for those patients with active COVID. People wanted to be treated, and they sought us out.

Patients wanted a doctor to do something—anything—to help them. They were grateful for the care they were getting. As the old saying goes, "People don't care how much you know; they care how much you care." My office was getting calls from as far away as Alaska. People wanted to make sure they were doing everything they could to beat this virus. They were asking for prevention protocols, and I obliged. It was the least I could do to restore hope and personal responsibility.

That summer was a busy one. We were trying to see as many patients as we possibly could. We added services such as IV fluid hydration for those having trouble keeping up. We were also running nebulizers pretty much nonstop for these patients. I made sure that everyone who needed one went home with a nebulizer. I utilized my new friend and colleague as a sounding board since he had treated hundreds of patients. It would not be long before I had one hundred patients. I saw how the disease is real. Some of my patients were really sick and had to be hospitalized. Despite my efforts, a few patients died.

However, in Texas the State Board of Pharmacy was interfering with our prescriptions being filled. It seems as though the pharmacy board would flag a doctor if certain drugs were being prescribed and alert the medical board. Now, mind you, the medical board is in place to monitor the proper licensing, credentials, and competency of physicians. What was worse, the medical board would then open an investigation on the physician, not because we harmed a patient but because we wrote a prescription!

These medications were FDA-approved, and doctors have authority to use off-label medications. A board investigation is a very scary thing for a doctor. This was the intimidation factor used to keep doctors from doing the right thing and doing their job—much to the detriment of patients. This wasn't fair to doctors or patients.

We found a Texas senator who was determined to help us. State senator Bob Hall began having Facebook Town Hall meetings to get the word out about doctors helping patients with COVID. I was honored to take part in one. Senator Hall also helped doctors in Texas with the pharmacy board and medical board issues. After all, we were fighting for our patients' lives during a pandemic.

Joining the Frontliners

It was about that time that I heard of America's Frontline Doctors. I can't begin to tell you how relieved I was to "find my people"! I felt like a turtle on a post—I had no idea how I got there, no idea where to go from there, and no way to get down, and no one was around to help. I missed the first White Coat Summit but watched as much as I could before the videos were taken off social media. I admired their courage, their integrity, their love of their patients, and most of all how they were upholding their oath. I chose to fly under the radar for a while, treating as many patients as I could. I was trying to get in as many patients as possible, running into late nights and ignoring my family, temporarily, for the greater good.

The media kept painting a gloom-and-doom picture, yet I saw a silver lining. The TV remained off most of the time; I couldn't handle the propaganda. I felt as though I were living a bad episode of *The Twilight Zone*. A lot of people felt the same way. I was checking our hospitalization rates as often as the updates came in (www.tmc.edu). What the news said and what the numbers on the local hospital tracking website said were very different. The only way I knew how to combat the fear and misleading information was by teaching people the truth using their own numbers against them. My social media live videos were my effort to set the record straight. I informed the American people how to discern the information on the website.

In the early fall the calls continued. The volume was down a bit, but I knew October was coming. October is always when respiratory diseases start to stack up. I had heard that the Frontline Doctors were going to meet in Washington, DC, again. I told my husband I just had to be there. I checked my schedule, moved a few patients around, and got a plane ticket to go. I needed to find physicians of like mind. I felt virtually alone on a little island, with few people to turn to. I needed to be among people who thought the same way I did—who cared about patients, knew what they were doing, and were doing the right thing.

I was absolutely giddy to meet these heroes. Initially I was a bundle of nerves because I thought maybe I wouldn't fit in.

I could not wait to meet Dr. Stella Immanuel and Dr. Simone Gold. I talked my friend Dr. Brian Procter into going too so I would know at least one person. I was so excited that I was no longer alone. We had a group chat joining us all together, making sure we all knew where to meet.

It was the most amazing time. It felt as though we had been friends forever: Dr. Shelley Cole, Dr. Richard Urso, Dr. Richard Eisner and Jane Eisner, Dr. Brian Tyson and Fabiola Tyson, Dr. Ben Marble, Dr. Robin Armstrong, Dr. Mark McDonald, Dr. Jeff Barke, Dr. Tom Reed, Dr. Lee Merritt, Dr. Simone Gold, and others. It was such a thrill to meet them face to face and maskless! Wow.

The conference was awesome. The information presented was what I had been searching for and could not find on my own. It was a breath of fresh air to finally get a scientific view that had real data and made sense. That evening, I was honored to get the official America's Frontline Doctors lab coat. It just didn't get any better than that.

SUPREME COURT STEPS

The press conference on the steps of the Supreme Court of the United States was mostly uneventful except for the heckling old man in University of Michigan attire. A friend of mine I hadn't seen in years drove in from Maryland to watch and posted the conference live on his Facebook page. One America News Network (OAN) was there broadcasting the press conference, interviewing some of the doctors with AFLDS. Dr. Court Koshar was there as a producer making a documentary with his longtime friend and director Adam Mariner. They set up a camera and interviewed a few of us after the press conference. I was honored to be asked my opinion based on a pediatrician's perspective. Me? Really? I was a newbie! More importantly, our message was going to be heard.

Then my phone started lighting up with messages from people I knew. People recognized me from a photo posted on social media. They were thrilled that I was one of *them*. I was now part of the elite group of doctors willing to do something to help save lives, America's Frontline Doctors. The message was getting out—for a few hours, at least. Then OAN's broadcast of the press conference was taken down. We were being censored! Social media blocked the pictures of us on the SCOTUS steps. Amazing.

I then realized that Dr. Stella Immanuel was in DC but missing from our group. Her absence was very noticeable. A few of us asked where Stella was, and soon it became apparent that she wasn't going to make it. I was really looking forward to meeting her in person. I had texted her back and forth a bit, mostly asking for her advice. I hoped I would bump into her somewhere that weekend.

We had been asked to be at the 1776 rally and were given an opportunity to speak. Patriots were everywhere—and so was Stella! I finally got to meet another one of my heroes. After the rally, we gathered for dinner. I fell in love with these people. I was on cloud nine. The only thing that would have topped it would have been if President Donald Trump himself walked up to us while we were eating at the Trump Hotel. That didn't happen, but I did not want it all to end.

Once I got home and back to business, I was more optimistic than ever. I had friends in the trenches with me, willing to help with tough medical issues, new therapies, the sharing of ideas, and morale boosting. I was not on my social media much because I was busy treating patients. Some of the patients had seen us on social media; some had heard from other patients. Word was spreading, and so was hope.

I contacted churches, offering to protect their staffs and congregations. My vision was to circle the wagons by protecting communities one church at a time. I felt very strongly I needed to help them bring hope, not fear. Some embraced the idea; others, including my home church, did not. "Fear not" was whispered to my soul over and over again.

Then something interesting happened. One day while walking and filming a live video, I noticed something strange. My video feed kept getting disrupted. I went through a checklist: Battery low? No. Wi-Fi disconnected? No. Loss of signal? No. Out of range? No. In fact, I looked up to see the cell tower very near to where I was standing. There was only one conclusion: I was being censored!

I tested my theory. The video I was filming was a discussion on how vaccines normally go through a process to be vetted for safety. I noted that if I mentioned a name such as Pfizer, Moderna, Johnson & Johnson, or any other vaccine company, my video would act as though it lost signal, and once it resumed, the spinning arrow would appear. I did this a few times until it became too annoying and explained to my audience that I was being censored and where they may find me in the near future.

I could not believe I had been targeted. I was an independent doctor in a small town. Why did anyone care what I thought? I shared my experience with my colleagues in a group text thread. No one was surprised. They all had been censored too. Some were in Facebook jail for months. One had her Twitter platform with thousands of followers taken down. It made me wonder, "Why are we such a threat? And to whom?" Many of the doctors with AFLDS regard censorship as a badge of honor.

TRAVELING TO BOOST FREEDOM

Word is getting out. The year 2021 has been one of my busiest years ever. It has also been one of the most frustrating and rewarding ones.

About six months after meeting Dr. Court Koshar and Adam Mariner near the SCOTUS steps, Dr. Koshar called to tell me the documentary film *Seeing 2020: The Censored Science of the COVID-19 Pandemic* was finished and being shown in small theater venues. It had been played in a small town in Texas, with Dr. Shelley Cole doing a Q and A afterward. Dr. Cole contacted me to see if I could do a road show in three more Texas cities where the documentary folks booked theaters. Since I was going to Dallas, I asked if I could invite my friend Dr. Peter McCullough.

The Dallas showing was very well attended, and Dr. McCullough's brilliance shone through. It was an honor to share the panel with him and Dr. Koshar. Dr. Brian Tyson, Dr. Stella Immanuel, and this man have done so much for our cause to get the word out about early outpatient treatment for COVID. Dr. McCullough subjected himself to criticism at Baylor University in Dallas because he published an article on outpatient treatment.[14] He's another hero of mine, speaking out on Fox shows with Tucker Carlson, Sean Hannity, and Laura Ingraham; on podcasts; on radio shows; and in print. I pinch myself knowing I have his cell number and can call him for advice anytime. He has a beautiful servant's heart. I don't know what I did to get the divine appointment to meet this man. I am so grateful for him.

Houston was next, and I shared the panel with two more brilliant people, Drs. Richard Urso and Robin Armstrong. Dr. Urso is a data machine. He can rattle off statistics and cite articles like few I have ever met. I think he rivals only Dr. McCullough on this. How in the world was I so blessed to meet this man? I am so out of my league. I have admired Dr. Armstrong ever since his stance on treating nursing home residents with hydroxychloroquine, which I have no doubt saved them. He was bashed by *Rolling Stone*, a monthly magazine that focuses on music, politics, and popular culture.[15] What does Hollywood know about medicine? They shredded Dr. Armstrong, but more surprisingly, the mainstream media ate it up. Here he was, a hero, but his lifesaving treatment was bashed and, worse, shunned by the medical community.

The last showing of the documentary took place in Georgetown, just outside Austin. Dr. Tom Reed and Sen. Bob Hall, the hero to Texas doctors, were with me. Dr. Koshar and Adam Mariner had to fly back to Arizona. What a great panel to be on. Senator Hall discussed what the public could do to support us, as well as what was on the political agenda regarding vaccine passports and mandates. Dr. Reed was brilliant in his delivery of the science behind air filtration in operating rooms so medical doctors and personnel don't pass out while wearing masks. He tackled the vaccine issues like a warrior, defining what a true vaccine is and does.

My thousand-mile weekend road trip was over. I was recharged being around these amazing people. Adam Mariner and Dr. Koshar did a phenomenal job on *Seeing 2020*.

GOING NATIONAL

Not long after my whirlwind weekend, I was asked to go to Ohio for more documentary presentations. Adam Mariner and I were heading this one. It was in Ohio that we met a naturopath from Florida, Jana Schmidt. She is awesome! She brought in the perspective of preventive health: Do you really need a vaccine if you eat right, exercise, and take care of yourself? This is such a foreign concept to Americans who are praising the idea of getting a vaccine, because they receive a free donut every day for a year, a burger and fries, beer, a lottery ticket for a chance to get an education, and so on. Have Americans lost their minds? I have seen doctors touting their donuts on social media. Since when do doctors promote a daily eating habit that contributes to one of the nastiest health issues we have: diabetes.

The people of the Cincinnati area welcomed us and embraced us. They are asking us to return. I can't wait! While in Ohio, I got a call from AFLDS asking me to join Dr. Simone Gold at her event The Uncensored Truth: Physicians and Patients Standing Up for Science, Freedom and Common Sense, in Stafford, Texas. I landed in Houston and had time to drive there, except my battery was dead. Not today, Satan! I was able to get a jump start and arrived in time to share the panel with Drs. Gold and Urso.[16] I am so blessed!

VACCINE CONCERNS

The vaccines have been worrying me for some time. Listening to Jana speak in Ohio really enforced these doubts. The speed to market was much faster than normal. The technology is new and has never been used this way before in humans. In the early phases of the trials, a serious neurological event or other serious medical event paused two of the four US trials.[17] In a different time, it would have halted the trials to ensure the safety of participants, and they would have gone back to animal studies. The way the Vaccine Adverse Event Reporting System (VAERS) data is ignored is simply mind-boggling.

In 1999 the rotavirus vaccine was pulled off the market due to fifteen cases of intussusception, a serious medical condition where the intestine telescopes on itself.[18] Sometimes it resolves on its own and sometimes a radiological procedure reduces it. The swine flu vaccine was pulled off the market when twenty-five deaths were reported.[19] Currently, not only are we now into thousands of deaths (4,328 as of July 14, 2021) and unexplained heart attacks, blood clots, strokes, and other severe neurological issues such as seizures, but there is a rush to vaccinate children under sixteen.[20] Why? They are buffers.

It makes no sense to vaccinate someone who recovered from the illness and is unaffected by the disease. This is beyond dangerous. It is unethical and unnecessary. I pray I am wrong, but only time will tell. I dread what we may find in our vaccinated population in the next few years. I am so afraid for the children who are being used in the experiment.

Keep in mind, these vaccines are being given under the Emergency Use Authorization. They were not FDA-approved as of this writing. These vaccines do not even fit the definition of a vaccine but are biological agents.

In my view, the VAERS data is not being reviewed by the appropriate entities to ensure the American people are protected.

I pray for the parents who may not know any better or think they are doing the world a great service. I pray the children have supernatural protection. I have spoken out to protect our patients. I testified at the Texas Senate Committee on State Affairs on May 6, 2021, to stop employer vaccine mandates and to not require vaccine passports (S.B. 1669). These actions are premature and discriminatory. The next target will be children. I have heard experts estimate that 50 percent of children are already immune to the SARS-CoV-2 virus, so why ruin their natural immunity? If they had chicken pox, they no longer require a varicella vaccine (for chicken pox). Why is COVID so different?

I will continue speaking out to protect the children. I speak as a pediatrician, a wife, and a mom. Never would I have thought I would be a spokesperson for America's Frontline Doctors as the pediatric director. What an honor and privilege to serve the American people! I have met some of the greatest people I could ever wish to know. God has put them in my path. I am thankful to them and embrace the purpose He has set forth for me. God has prepared me and each of us for such a time as this.

Chapter 13

WHY WE CARE

Adapted from the book *The Luciferian Strategy*
by Mary Ann Levy[1]

J ESUS SAID IN Matthew 24:36–37, "But of that day and hour
no one knows, not even the angels of heaven, but My Father
only. *But as the days of Noah were, so also will the coming
of the Son of Man be*" (NKJV, emphasis added). In the days of
Noah, the Nephilim were on the earth. These were the product
of unions between the "sons of God" and the "daughters of
men....Those were the mighty men who were of old, men of
renown" (Gen. 6:4, NKJV).

Why do we care if there were giants or fallen angels? First,
we care for truth's sake. We care because the distortion and
perversion of creation has not stopped. We care because if we
are not aware of the schemes of the enemy, if we ignore him,
as past generations have, then we empower him.

If information points to the Bible's narrative as being accurate, the elitists don't want it propagated. If it goes against
Darwinian evolution, it's not to be spoken. Professors, archae-
ologists, and others have lost their tenure and positions for
daring to speak the truth.

We care because to sit at ease in our lives, caught up with

the affairs of this life only as they regard us, blinds us to the scheme of things around us. Our Father God is moving heaven and earth to try to get truth to earth's inhabitants, but many ignore the truth because it makes them uncomfortable. Then suddenly, seemingly without warning, disaster strikes. The following scripture in Amos speaks to this mindset.

> What sorrow awaits you who lounge in luxury in Jerusalem, and you who feel secure in Samaria! You are famous and popular in Israel, and people go to you for help. But go over to Calneh and see what happened there. Then go to the great city of Hamath and down to the Philistine city of Gath. You are no better than they were, and look at how they were destroyed. You push away every thought of coming disaster, but your actions only bring the day of judgment closer. How terrible for you who sprawl on ivory beds and lounge on your couches, eating the meat of tender lambs from the flock and of choice calves fattened in the stall. You sing trivial songs to the sound of the harp and fancy yourselves to be great musicians like David. You drink wine by the bowlful and perfume yourselves with fragrant lotions. You care nothing about the ruin of your nation. Therefore, you will be the first to be led away as captives. Suddenly, all your parties will end.
>
> —AMOS 6:1–7, NLT

This scripture was speaking to Israel at the time, but the same mindset is prevalent today in mankind.

We care because we were given forewarning when Jesus said:

> When the Son of Man comes, it will be the same as when Noah lived. In the days before the flood, people were eating and drinking. They were marrying and being given in marriage. This kept on until the day Noah went into the large boat. They did not know what was happening until the

flood came and the water carried them all away. It will be like this when the Son of Man comes.

—MATTHEW 24:37–39, NLV

We've looked at the condition of the earth in the days of Noah when fallen angels were ruling as gods and their offspring were ravaging mankind, when fallen angels were exchanging the knowledge of good and evil with mankind for servitude.

We are warned:

The thing that hath been, it is that which shall be; and that which is done is that which shall be done: and there is no new thing under the sun. Is there any thing whereof it may be said, See, this is new? it hath been already of old time, which was before us. There is no remembrance of former things; neither shall there be any remembrance of things that are to come with those that shall come after.

—ECCLESIASTES 1:9–11

We care because we don't have to fall subservient to this scheme. We *can* be equipped to "resist the devil and he will flee" (Jas. 4:7). Jesus Himself said, when the seventy returned whom He had sent against the enemy in His day:

And the seventy returned again with joy, saying, Lord, even the devils are subject unto us through thy name.

And he said unto them, I beheld Satan as lightning fall from heaven. Behold, I give unto you power to tread on serpents and scorpions, and over all the power of the enemy: and nothing shall by any means hurt you. Notwithstanding in this rejoice not, that the spirits are subject unto you; but rather rejoice, because your names are written in heaven.

—LUKE 10:17–20

Understanding that "serpents and scorpions" were metaphors for various types of the enemy, we can see Jesus never intended His own to be the hapless victims of the enemy. Yes, there are those called to martyrdom, but others are to exercise the authority bequeathed to believers. Understand that just as our government cannot give military-grade weapons to untrained, uncommitted civilians, neither can our Father God entrust His authority and weaponry to those who are not in submission to Him. The seven sons of Sceva learned this lesson:

> But certain also of the strolling Jews, exorcists, took upon them to name over them that had the evil spirits the name of the Lord Jesus, saying, I adjure you by Jesus whom Paul preacheth. And there were seven sons of one Sceva, a Jew, a chief priest, who did this. And the evil spirit answered and said unto them, Jesus I know, and Paul I know: but who are ye? And the man in whom the evil spirit was leaped on them, and mastered both of them, and prevailed against them, so that they fled out of that house naked and wounded.
> —ACTS 19:13–16, ASV

Our position is based upon our relationship. It's not a matter of favoritism; it's a matter of the heart of surrender. Just as Shadrach, Meshach, and Abednego declared centuries ago, in Daniel 3:16–18 (NIV):

> Shadrach, Meshach and Abednego replied to him, "King Nebuchadnezzar, we do not need to defend ourselves before you in this matter. If we are thrown into the blazing furnace, the God we serve is able to deliver us from it, and he will deliver us from Your Majesty's hand. But even if he does not, we want you to know, Your Majesty, that we will not serve your gods or worship the image of gold you have set up."

We see from this that they fully *knew* God was *able* to deliver them and ultimately *would* deliver them from the king's hand—even if that meant in death. They *knew* they were not given over to this king. Even if they were to be devoured by the flames, it would not alter their relationship with their God. And after walking in the fire with them, God was able to save them from the fiery furnace.

So many base their relationship with God on their circumstances. If they go through tragedy and difficulty, and they pray and the difficulty does not go away, they walk away from the Lord and choose to believe He either doesn't care or doesn't exist. Their relationship is circumstantial, whereas our Father's relationship with us says, "I will *never* leave you, nor will I *ever* forsake you." (See Hebrews 13:5.) Just as in a marriage we vow to one another "for better or for worse, in sickness and in health," there's *commitment*—without which we have a one-sided "relationship." We cannot fully participate in all the aspects of a relationship with God if we are in a conditional relationship that says, "Well, I'll believe if You do such and such," or, "I *did* believe until..." Faith, believing, isn't a matter of just believing God is and that Jesus is His Son. Scripture tells us even demons believe this—because they *do* know the truth. Remember the enemy in the wilderness tempting Jesus with Scripture? James 2:19–20 (ASV) says:

> Thou believest that God is one; thou doest well: the demons also believe, and shudder. But wilt thou know, O vain man, that faith apart from works is barren?

Jesus *knew* Scripture—but it's not a matter of *knowing*; it's a matter of submitting to the truth. It's a matter of believing God to be who He says He is and who He has shown Himself to be at the cross of Christ. At Calvary, God demonstrated and proved His love to mankind by so greatly loving and dearly prizing the world that He gave His only Son. No one extracted or demanded that giving; God knew it was the only way to bring mankind back into relationship with Him, so He voluntarily gave.

There are many today in various doctrines who have given away much of their authority over the enemy. They believe and are in relationship with the Father, and when they die, they will be with Him, but while here on earth, they have relinquished much of their authority over sickness and the enemy's attacks. As long as we draw breath, we need to be pressing in to know more of this unfathomable God!

Likewise, God has forewarned us of the realities of the last days, but we are challenged to believe what He has said. When "sudden destruction" comes upon the earth, where even the very elect will be deceived, we are challenged to be prepared. (See 1 Thessalonians 5:3 and Matthew 24:24.) We care about the truths of history and their relevance to today because we want to be trained and equipped so we don't have this sudden destruction fall upon us unawares.

It has been said, "Who controls the past...controls the future."[2] The Luciferian Strategy as lived out through his agents is to hide and distort true history so they can determine our future. However, the truth is that we *can* occupy until Jesus returns. (See Luke 19:13.) We *can* live and move and have our being in Him, living with all authority over all the works of the enemy—and *nothing* shall by any means harm us. We are not to live in fear of the enemy and what he is bringing on the earth. We can live in total confidence, as Shadrach, Meshach, and Abednego did, that our God is able

and will deliver us. Yes, they spent a night in a fiery furnace—
I can only imagine the experience—but they were not alone.
Nor will those of us be who live in the last days as we exercise
our God-given authority over all the works of the enemy!

PART III

IN 2015, WHEN I was a local doctor and minister in Houston and virtually nobody nationwide had heard my name, I was moved by the Spirit of God to write a prophetic warning to America. What I have written in this section is the result of that burden. I had read a disturbing plan, apparently laid out many decades ago, to disciple America away from God, remove its Christian foundations, and train society and its children in wickedness. I knew we needed to be even more strategic in our plan to bring America back to God.

I say to those who feel they have a prophetic burden from the Lord for their nation, family, or city—be encouraged to speak your message boldly, even if nobody knows your name. God will raise you up in due time and exalt you to speak from an even greater platform, for His glory. My life and what you will read in the following pages are evidence of that.

May it bless, convict, and inspire you to engage in our times more than ever before, discipling America back to God.

Chapter 14

MY BURDEN FOR AMERICA

MY HEART IS heavy as I see the senseless killings, the pain, and the evil in the eyes of the perpetrators. Call it the burden of being a prophet, but I feel the pain of the victims and the helplessness and hopelessness of our people. I feel the grief of a Savior who died for us and was made sin so we could be righteous, a Savior who gave His life so we could be free. The victims are not only those killed but the families of the killers, who will forever live with the guilt and shame of "my kid did that."

Most importantly, I feel the frustrations of a nation reaping the evil it has craved for and sown but not recognizing that this is payback.

Oh, America!

Our country was a land dedicated to God from its foundations but has turned away from the very foundation that gave it the audacity to become the greatest nation in the world. Our country is a city on a hill that has turned from light to darkness.

America has craved for evil and opened its gates to it. America has driven God out of its public and social life and given evil free rein.

We have propagated evil through our television shows and

movies and carried out the agendas of hell. We have sacrificed our children to Molek through abortion and brought in abominations through legalizing perversions. We now celebrate evil and despise and persecute good.

My heart bleeds every day as I see children on hard medicines for ADHD and behavioral problems. As beautiful as my job is as a pediatrician, I feel the helplessness of parents looking at me and to drugs to combat the craziness of their children. I see them zoned out on their phones and tablets, playing the very demonic games that have brought all this craziness into their minds. I see parents in denial of the effect on their children because they themselves are a product of the same craziness.

As a deliverance minister, I see the mind-boggling oppression and demonic harassment on children of God. They come from all over the world to our center for deliverance, looking up to Dr. Stella to lay hands on them, wave a magic wand, and end the torment they are going through. I see the kind of demonic harassment that could only be found in horror movies. The boldness of these creatures to torment and harass even the elect! I feel the frustration of trying to lead them to Jesus, the only person who can deliver them, but the enemy has a choke hold on their minds, blocking the very prerequisites for their deliverance, which are humility, godly sorrow, and deep repentance. I feel the frustration of trying to bring people to the place of deep repentance that brings down the mercy of God, because we have been robbed of the gift of repentance from years of doctrinal programming. I see them struggle with accepting that they are mere humans. As King David said in Psalm 103:13–16 (ESV),

Like as a father pitieth his children, so the LORD pitieth them that fear him. For he knoweth our frame; he remembereth that we are dust. As for man, his days are as grass; as a flower of the field, so he flourisheth. For the wind passeth over it, and it is gone; and the place thereof shall know it no more.

I feel great compassion as I see individuals fighting personal battles that never end. I see families torn apart, terror and fear on every side. And I see the weariness of men and women of God as it becomes more difficult to be true to the Word without being labeled a hater. I see more and more sinners come into the church and demand to be accommodated in their sin. How the hearts of true men and women of God bleed as they realize more and more the compromises they have to make to keep their ministries alive.

I am wondering when, as a nation, we will repent and cry out to God to help us. I desire to see a desperation for God like the saints of old had. I know some religious spirit is rising up in someone right now with indignation, as if to say, "How can you say that when we have prayed for twenty, thirty, fifty years for revival?" Are we saying we have done our part and God has not done His? Are we now more righteous than our Maker? Is God unfaithful in His promises?

Saints, we all agree that something needs to be done, but it looks as if we lack the spiritual capacity and fortitude to do anything. We are fighting the individual battles that will have no end, because as long as America, our great land, is sick, it will affect us all. Saints, the shootings, the killings, the financial turmoil, the tornadoes, the hurricanes, and so on are all part of the shaking.

I watch the shows with the blood moons and prophetic

predictions and on-target analyses of the Word and what is to come, but I don't see our great men and women of God leading people to repentance. I even watch great men of God from other nations preach heartbreaking messages, and they end with clapping and standing ovations. When are we going to repent, saints? Messages that when preached in other parts of the world will have the crowd on their faces crying for hours elicit applause in America, celebrating the speaker for a job well done.

We have craved for evil or turned a blind eye as the world pushes us into the closet as we chase our elusive breakthroughs, purposes, and next levels.

Second Chronicles 7:14 says, "If my people, which are called by my name, shall humble themselves, and pray, and seek my face, and turn from their wicked ways; then will I hear from heaven, and will forgive their sin, and will heal their land."

When are we going to humble ourselves? When will our hearts break for our sins, the sins of our land, and the sins of our leaders? When are we going to be desperate?

Oh, that God will give us broken and contrite hearts—not lip service but true brokenness, a desperation that touches the very throne of God to release the power necessary for transformation. Oh, that He will give us the capacity to pray and travail to the point of breaking through.

We had a prayer conference at our revival center in Houston. As we prayed and cried out, my heart was so heavy and broken that I sobbed uncontrollably—but everyone else was standing up and doing the "O God, O God!" thing. And the Holy Spirit spoke that the hearts of the people are hard and unbroken. Even as the prophetic word came pouring out amid my sobbing, the people still could not be broken. Saints, when our hearts break, when we turn from our wicked ways, when we drop our humanism or self-aggrandizement, when we allow God to break down our pride, when we realize that only God can fix the mess we have created and He will hear only the prayer of the humble, we will cry out for the gift of repentance. If we don't, judgment is coming, and it will start in the house of God. Maybe we will wait till the persecution intensifies.

> *O God, help America! O Lord, have mercy on America, our beloved country. Jesus, please don't leave us to our own devices. Draw us to a place of deep repentance, Lord, that we may cry out for our nation, in Jesus' name.*

A FIGHT FOR THE SOUL OF AMERICA IS A FIGHT FOR THE WORLD

Saints, how long will we watch while the world system takes over and pushes us into the closet? Every fiber of Christianity is under attack in this nation. The onslaught on the church is tremendous, and people are beginning to feel there is no hope.

Many of us are under siege, with one battle after another in our homes, families, businesses, health, and so on. We are fighting personal battles while ignoring the greater battle for our nation. When there is evil in the land, it affects everybody. Just as we Christians are priests unto the Lord, so too the unbelievers are priests unto the devil. They seem to be very busy in promoting their agenda and terrorizing anyone who dares to disagree.

The truth is that the church is to blame for the moral decline in our nation because we failed to watch our spiritual gates. For years we have danced to the tune of "Catch your breakthrough, your purpose, your next level." We have ignored the Great Commission in Matthew.

Where were we when they took prayer out of schools or the Ten Commandments out of the court system? This has not been a random accident. The devil and his priesthood have carefully planned the current state while the church chased its breakthrough. This deception has crept up unobserved on so many people. It can best be demonstrated through the well-known analogy of a frog in a pot of water. If you put a frog in a pot of boiling water, it is smart enough to know that it is in terrible danger and will immediately jump out to safety. But if you turn up the heat very slowly, it doesn't notice the changes that are taking place and will slowly cook to death.

Many people today are slowly cooking to death and don't seem to realize how far they have come from where they once were. The Lord has sent warning after warning to His church in America, but we ignored those prophets. We called them names, doomsday prophets, haters, and so on. There has been a deliberate plan to turn America away from God, but we can fight for the soul of this nation through prayer. In the following chapters I include several prayer plans that we as the body of Christ can use to disciple this nation and turn America back to God.

Chapter 15

TEN-POINT PLAN TO DISCIPLE AMERICA BACK TO GOD

I READ WHAT PURPORTED to be a ten-point plan[1] for the destruction of Christianity and the establishment of a new world order. This plan, which also claimed to be nearly seventy years in the making, was said to have been crafted by an occultist to rid nations of all Christian traditions. Its points were so specific and troubling that I want to list some of them.

A DEMON-INSPIRED PLAN

1. Take God and prayer out of the educational system.

This plan intended to change curricula to ensure that children were "freed from the bondage of Christian culture." It stated that with God out of education, children would naturally conclude that God is not a necessary part of life. Instead, children would focus on those things the school counted as worthy and would look into alternatives such as Transcendental Meditation, which takes children into altered states of consciousness to meet with demons, or "spirit guides," as they are called in new age spirituality.

2. Reduce parental authority over the children.

The plan was to break communication between parent and child so parents would not pass down Christian traditions. The specific steps included

- promoting the rights of children to tell parents and teachers, "I have my rights. You cannot talk to me like that";

- abolishing corporal punishment;

- turning teachers into agents of implementation to tell children, "Your parent has no right to force you to pray or read the Bible. You are yourself and have rights of your own. You need self-expression, self-realization, self-fulfillment."

3. Destroy the Judeo-Christian family structure or the traditional Christian family structure.

This plan brazenly stated that the family is oppressive, and "if you break the family, you break the nation. Liberate the people from the confines of this structure." Steps included

- promoting sexual promiscuity—freeing young people to have premarital sex. The plan was to lift "free sex" so high that the joy of it was seen as the highest fulfillment in life, making everybody proud to be seen as sexually active.

- using advertising and media, TV, magazines, and the film industry to promote sexual enjoyment as the highest pleasure in humanity. Of course, today almost every advertisement includes a sexual connotation. Nearly every product is advertised with seductive women and imagery.

4. If sex is free, then make abortion legal and easy.

The plan wickedly promoted building clinics for abortion—called "health clinics"—in schools. It stated, "If people are going to enjoy the joy of sexual relationships, they need to be free of unnecessary fears; in other words they should not be hampered with unwanted pregnancies. Abortion as told by Christians is oppressive and denies our rights. We have a right to choose whether we want to have a child or not. If a woman does not want the pregnancy, she should have the freedom to get rid of that pregnancy painlessly and as easily as possible."

Of course, today abortion is not only accessible but sometimes forced on people and is seen by some as a strategy to curb population growth.

5. Make divorce easy and legal. Free people from the concept of marriage for life.

To break the bond of love between a husband and wife, the plan was to promote easy, no-guilt divorces. The author even exalted this idea of divorce as a way to shed one love that was dying and allow a new love to come forth. This directly contradicts God's Word, which says in Malachi 2:16, "For the LORD God of Israel says that He hates divorce" (NKJV).

6. Make homosexuality an alternative lifestyle.

Of course, this wicked plan encouraged any and all sexualities, including homosexuality, incest, and bestiality. According to the Bible, this is an abomination before the eyes of God.

> Thou shalt not lie with mankind, as with womankind: it is abomination.
>
> —LEVITICUS 18:22

If a man also lie with mankind, as he lieth with a woman, both of them have committed an abomination: they shall surely be put to death; their blood shall be upon them.

—LEVITICUS 20:13

7. Debase art; make it run mad.

The plan envisioned new forms of art that would corrupt and defile the imagination of people. We have seen that happen beyond anyone's imagination.

8. Use media to promote an antichrist agenda and change mindsets.

The plan involved using the power of media to turn minds and attitudes against God and the message of the church. This was long before social media, round-the-clock news channels, and the rise of cancel culture.

9. Create an interfaith movement.

The plan was to put other faiths on par with Christianity and pull Christianity down to the level of "just another faith." This also promoted humanism, which puts man in the middle of any religion as the one who gets to decide what is true and what is not, rather than submitting to almighty God.

10. Get governments to make all these laws, and get the church to endorse these changes.

The plan actually envisioned that churches would change their doctrine and accommodate wicked laws promulgated by governments.

When I read this plan, I was grieved by how much of it has already come to pass. How can the devil's people have so much foresight and planning while God's church sleeps and society is debased?

God's Ten-Point Plan

This ten-point plan was given to me by the Holy Spirit on May 9, 2015. We had been praying for America at our church for several months, five to seven hours every day from Monday through Saturday. We greatly felt the burden of the current state of the church and nation and a helplessness of not knowing what to do. We came to the conclusion that only God can help us, and for weeks we planned to just cry out for help.

As we cried one day to the Lord, I felt His presence so heavy on me, and He began to download these revelations into my spirit. If the devil had a plan and it succeeded, we can have a plan too to turn the tide of things. The Bible says we should go into the world and make disciples of every nation. So I picked up a pen and started writing frantically as the Holy Spirit ministered to me, giving me a ten-point plan to disciple America back to God. This can be done in any nation, with any individuals or groups of people.

My prayer is that people will adopt whatever part they can do. I know a lot of men and women of God are already doing many parts of this plan and much more. But I'm going to put it down the way the Lord gave it to me.

We have also included targeted prayer points to help direct your praying if you need it.

1. Put prayer back into the fabric of America.

- Raise up prayer warriors in schools by teaching children to start student-led prayer meetings in schools.

- Raise up prayer warriors in prisons through prison ministries.

- Teach people to start personal, family, and church altars of prayer.

Teach children about deep prayer warfare and how to enjoy the presence of God. Children should be taught how to recognize sin in the schools and to bring repentance before God.

One of our daughters here in the church came back to tell us that the leadership of her school had brought in a lady who wrote books on magic to give a talk at their school. She proceeded to tell her friends that it was witchcraft. She then sat in the class and under her breath prayed for the minds of all the children not to be influenced. She covered the whole class with the blood of Jesus and prayed all through the lecture. She also bound the spirits behind the lady and said that they would not operate in her school. She was only eleven years old, but she had been taught to recognize the works of the devil and take authority over them.

Our children need to see us fasting, praying, and crying out so they can learn from experience. We should not put them in children's church to play or leave them at home when going to church. That's what Pharaoh told Moses. "Go to the wilderness and worship your God, and don't leave the children behind" (Exod. 10:24).

The difference between regular quiet time and true prayer altar time is in breaking into the presence of God. A lot of us pray without actually getting into His presence. We need to practice spending time in God's presence and teach our children to know the presence of God and learn what it takes to break into that presence.

2. Teach children how to respect themselves and authority from school-led groups.

If we train our children to realize that their lives are precious in the sight of God and their destinies can be derailed by poor choices, they will make good choices most of the time. We have children in their twenties who have chosen to preserve themselves and stay undefiled because they were taught to recognize that their lives are precious and God has a plan for them. We can show them examples of grown-ups and the mess they got into because of defilement and premarital sex.

3. Support marriages in prayer and get marriage counselors and churches to teach the biblical stand on marriage.

Marriage is one of the most corrupted institutions in this nation. Many people are suffering today because of wrong marital foundations. We need to teach the biblical pattern of courtship. We need to let our children know that dating is not scriptural but a distraction from their destiny and dreams. If they are not ripe for marriage, there is no need for a boyfriend or girlfriend. Courtship should be a premarital process done with chaperones and involve their spiritual leaders and much prayer. I tell people all the time that hell is the only thing worse than a bad marriage. If you as a child of God marry an unbeliever, your father-in-law is the devil and he will treat you accordingly. It is important to encourage purity programs among youths.

4. Teach abstinence and get pro-life organizations to provide support for life and adoption programs.

A lot of organizations are already doing this.

5. Raise up deliverance ministers, counselors, and prayer support for those who want to come out of the gay lifestyle and for Christians struggling with sexual immorality.

Many people who have been afflicted by the homosexual demon are under bondage, especially Christians who find themselves struggling with this. We have to provide solutions to this challenge as a church—not judge them and throw out,

"Thou shalt not lie with mankind," but provide deliverance. Bring down the presence of God, which can change things and deliver them completely.

We also need those struggling with these weaknesses to know that you don't give up that struggle and let the devil win. Many people are struggling with some other sins and are fighting the good fight of faith. There is overcoming to do, and we must resist the devil and put him to shame. We don't submit to and glamorize the sin.

6. Mobilize people to fast for the nation.

- Every Christian should fast for a day for America. You can choose any day of the week. If thousands of us do that, there will come a time when many will be praying and fasting for the nation daily.

- Adopt a state in America to pray for daily, that God's hand may be upon it.

- Mobilize America to bring repentance to God for our sins. Deep, godly sorrow leads to genuine repentance.

7. Get Americans to read the Bible or listen to audio Bible apps as they drive, and so on.

One way to get a good knowledge of Scripture is to read it every day. Get into the habit of listening to the Word of God.

- Play it on your app on your phone.

- Listen to it as you drive to work, while you are cooking in the kitchen, or as you are doing household chores.

- Have the audio Bible play in your house, office, and church when you are not there, and let it charge your environment.

- Let it play at a low volume in your children's rooms as they sleep instead of television, and it will minister to their spirits as they sleep.

- Have the Bible instead of music play on your phone waiting tone at your business.

It's amazing the presence of God that can be cultivated in an area just by letting Scripture play there. Let's get the Word of God back into our lives so it can bring life back to us. I use Bible Gateway online and play it on my computer and smartphones, including when I travel.

8. Locate Christians in leadership and government, and support them in prayer.

- Raise up prayer warriors to pray for government officials.

- Pray to reverse the evil laws that have been passed.

- Raise up prayer warriors to pray for Hollywood and influence what comes out of it.

- Raise up serious prayer covers for popular people the enemy is using to foster his agenda that they may get saved or be silenced.

9. Get local churches to bring repentance before God on behalf of our nation and pray for it whenever they meet for other purposes.

- Pray for pastors and ministers to be relevant to God's agenda in this season.

- Train deliverance ministers and prayer warriors to support local churches.

- Encourage local churches to send their prayer warriors for free training.

- Support local churches and ministers through prayer, especially against the spirit of deception and for God to speak through them.

- Deal with the ruling spirits in all situations that are contrary to God's Word, including false religions, and pull them down (see Ephesians).

- Pray for the lost.

- Use the seven-point prayer in the next chapter to charge your environment with fire.

10. Raise awareness through media and social media.

As you read this, help to distribute it. Post it on your social media. Order copies for your bookstore, church, and local distribution outlet. We have videos on this message on our YouTube channel. Watch them and share them. God will help us get the message out, in Jesus' name.

Chapter 16

PROPHETIC PRAYER POINTS

I N THE NEXT several pages, I present sets of brief prayer points written by me and others. These are prayers that my church and I pray, and we ask you to join with us in making these powerful prophetic statements over our land. I believe God is already answering them and will continue to answer them as more of us cry out for solutions to national problems so big that no man can solve them.

In addition to the declarations I wrote, I included some written by people I greatly respect in ministry. You can feel their hearts through the prayers, and I know they will ignite your soul with fresh zeal to see God's Spirit move powerfully in our world. Bless you as you agree with us in these prophetic prayer points.

SEVEN-POINT PRAYER TO CHARGE YOUR ENVIRONMENT WITH FIRE AND OPEN THE HEAVENS

By Dr. Stella Immanuel

If revival is going to visit a nation, it starts with the people—with you and me. Spend quality time in praise and worship. Bring quality repentance for your sins, even the unknown ones. Ask for forgiveness and mercy before you start praying.

Spend at least one minute on each prayer point. Pray in the Spirit to close.

> Oh that thou wouldest rend the heavens, that thou wouldest come down, that the mountains might flow down at thy presence, as when the melting fire burneth, the fire causeth the waters to boil, to make thy name known to thine adversaries, that the nations may tremble at thy presence!
>
> —ISAIAH 64:1–2

> But to which of the angels said he at any time, Sit on my right hand, until I make thine enemies thy footstool? Are they not all ministering spirits, sent forth to minister for them who shall be heirs of salvation?
>
> —HEBREWS 1:13–14

> The angel of the Lord encampeth round about them that fear him, and delivereth them.
>
> —PSALM 34:7

1. O God, arise and charge my life with Your fire in the name of Jesus.

2. O God, arise and charge this environment with fire—the building, the trees, the animals and insects, and everything in this environment with the Holy Ghost fire.

3. We charge the heavens over this place, over this neighborhood, city, state, and nation with the Holy Ghost fire in the name of Jesus.

4. O God, arise and rend the heavens and come down in Your power, Your fire, Your anointing, in the name of Jesus.

5. We send the blood of Jesus and the fire of the Holy Ghost into the foundation of this compound, building, neighborhood, city, and so on, and purify it in the name of Jesus.

6. We call for the host of heaven, warrior angels, and ministering spirits to appear, fight for us, fight with us, minister to us, and deliver us in Jesus' name.

7. Holy Spirit, we welcome You. Visit us today, Lord. The Spirit of power and might, breath of the living God, overshadowing presence of God, power of the highest, the Spirit of grace and supplication, and so much more.

SEVEN-DAY PRAYER FOR PERSONAL REVIVAL

By Dr. Stella Immanuel

Pray this daily for seven days, with some fasting, and watch the fire ignite in you. Share your testimony of what God is doing in you as you press in. May His refreshing presence and power visit you, in Jesus' name.

Lord, thou hast been favourable unto thy land: thou hast brought back the captivity of Jacob. Thou hast forgiven the iniquity of thy people, thou hast covered all their sin. Selah.

Thou hast taken away all thy wrath: thou hast turned thyself from the fierceness of thine anger. Turn us, O God of our salvation, and cause thine anger toward us to cease. Wilt thou be angry with us for ever? wilt thou draw out thine anger to all generations? Wilt thou not revive us again: that thy people may rejoice in thee? Shew us thy mercy, O LORD, and grant us thy salvation. I will hear what God the LORD will speak: for he will speak peace unto his people, and to his saints: but let them not turn again to folly. Surely his salvation is nigh them that fear him; that glory may dwell in our land. Mercy and truth are met together; righteousness and peace have kissed each other. Truth shall spring out of the earth; and righteousness shall look down from heaven. Yea, the Lord shall give that which is good; and our land shall yield her increase. Righteousness shall go before him; and shall set us in the way of his steps.

—PSALM 85

O God, why hast thou cast us off for ever? why doth thine anger smoke against the sheep of thy pasture? Remember thy congregation, which thou hast purchased of old; the rod of thine inheritance, which thou hast redeemed; this mount Zion, wherein thou hast dwelt. Lift up thy feet unto the perpetual desolations; even all that the enemy hath done wickedly in the sanctuary. Thine enemies roar in the midst of thy congregations; they set up their ensigns for signs. A man was famous according as he had lifted up axes upon the thick trees. But now they break down the carved work thereof at once with axes and hammers. They have cast fire into thy sanctuary, they have defiled by casting down the dwelling place of thy name to the ground. They said in their hearts, Let us destroy them together: they have burned up all the synagogues of God in the land. We see not our signs: there is no more any prophet: neither is there among us any that knoweth how long. O God, how long shall the adversary reproach? shall the enemy blaspheme thy name for ever? Why withdrawest thou thy hand, even thy right hand? pluck it out of thy bosom. For God is my King of old, working salvation in the midst of the earth.

Thou didst divide the sea by thy strength: thou brakest the heads of the dragons in the waters. Thou brakest the heads of leviathan in pieces, and gavest him to be meat to the people inhabiting the wilderness. Thou didst cleave the fountain and the flood: thou driedst up mighty rivers. The day is thine, the night also is thine: thou hast prepared the light and the sun. Thou hast set all the borders of the earth: thou hast made summer and winter. Remember this, that the enemy hath reproached, O Lord, and that the foolish people have blasphemed thy name. O deliver not the soul of thy turtledove unto the multitude of the wicked: forget not the congregation of thy poor for ever. Have respect unto the covenant: for the dark places of the earth are full of the habitations of cruelty. O let not the oppressed return ashamed: let the poor and needy praise thy name. Arise, O God, plead thine own cause: remember how the foolish man reproacheth thee daily. Forget not the voice of thine enemies: the tumult of those that rise up against thee increaseth continually.

—PSALM 74

PRAYER POINTS

- Father, teach me to be the true bride of Christ, in Jesus' name.

- Lord Jesus, cause my heart to pursue You.

- Draw me by Your right hand of righteousness, in the name of Jesus.

- Father, remove all distractions that are keeping me away from You, in the name of Jesus.

- Father, give me a hunger and desperation in my heart for You.

- Open the book of remembrance for me, O Lord.

- The Word says a broken and contrite spirit You will not despise. Teach me to recognize my unworthiness and to come to You in humility and brokenness.

- Draw us as a people and nation into Your presence. Don't leave us the way we are, O God of our salvation.

- Your kingdom come, O Lord, and let Your will be done in my life as it is written in heaven.

- Our hearts are cold, Lord Jesus. Touch and melt our hearts and set them on fire for You.

- Father, awaken our slumbering spirits from the comforts and enchantments that have held us down, in the name of Jesus.

- Save and deliver us from our weaknesses and sins, in Jesus' name.

- Anoint us with humility and brokenness.

- Deliver us from all the reasons and excuses we give for not pursuing You.

- Lord Jesus, mold us after Your loving image.

- Lord, give us Your wisdom and guidance that we might do Your will.

- Place Your heart within our hearts, and set us apart for You, O Lord.

- Cause Your Word through me to be more effective than ever, in Jesus' name.

- Equip my life to accomplish things far beyond my imagination, things I see as impossible for me today.

- My Father, give me and my children dreams that will change our lives.

- Serpents and scorpions in my blood, die, in the name of Jesus.

- Anything that is inside of me resisting God, come out and die, in Jesus' name.

- Anything quenching the fire of God in my life, come out now and go one way to the pit, in Jesus' name.

- Proverbs 1:23–28 says that if God speaks and we do not obey, He will not answer our prayers. Father, teach us to obey You, in Jesus' name.

- Father, help us to be revived with Your principles and values of righteousness, love, and justice.

- Power from on high, fall. Power that cannot be insulted by the kingdom of darkness, fall upon my life, in Jesus' name.

- Father, increase my spiritual capacity, in the name of Jesus, capacity to pray, to fast, to read the Word, to be obedient.

- Lord, work in our hearts.

- Father, give us Your heart for the city.

- O righteous Father, we pray that You would give the community Your heart.

PRAYER TO DESTROY THE COVENS OF DARKNESS

By Dr. Stella Immanuel

This prayer is for people who believe there is a witchcraft or satanic gang-up against their lives and destiny. If you feel that witchcraft manipulation is being used against you, you need to arise with holy anger and scatter the covens of darkness harassing your life. The only language the enemy understands is violence, and you will win, in Jesus' name.

> Thou art my battle axe and weapons of war: for with thee will I break in pieces the nations, and with thee will I destroy kingdoms.
>
> —JEREMIAH 51:20

> Behold, I will make thee a new sharp threshing instrument having teeth: thou shalt thresh the mountains, and beat them small, and shalt make the hills as chaff.
>
> —ISAIAH 41:15

> Associate yourselves, O ye people, and ye shall be broken in pieces; and give ear, all ye of far countries: gird yourselves, and ye shall be broken in pieces; gird yourselves, and ye shall be broken in pieces. Take counsel together, and it shall come to nought; speak the word, and it shall not stand: for God is with us. For the LORD spake thus to me with a strong hand, and instructed me that I should not walk in the way of this people, saying, Say ye not, A confederacy, to all them to whom this people shall say, A confederacy; neither fear ye their fear, nor be afraid.
>
> Sanctify the LORD of hosts himself; and let him be your fear, and let him be your dread. And he shall be for a sanctuary; but for a stone of stumbling and for a rock of offence to both the houses of Israel, for a gin and for a snare to the inhabitants of Jerusalem. And many among them shall stumble, and fall, and be broken, and be snared, and be taken. Bind up the testimony, seal the law among my disciples.
>
> —ISAIAH 8:9–16

Repent before God before you start.

PRAYER POINTS

- Arise, O God, and make me your battle-ax. Make me a sharp threshing instrument.

- Every coven gathering for my sake in the air, in the waters, in the earth, in the forest, stumble, stumble, stumble, in the name of Jesus.

- Every power blocking my life, my destiny, my ministry, fall from your high places, in Jesus' name.

- Every marine or witchcraft coven gathered to bring me down, be broken, be broken, be broken, in Jesus' name.

- Every snare set by my foundation, catch your owners, in Jesus' name.

- Any power, any spirit, any personality, any person that refuses to let me go, be crushed into powder by the rock of ages, in Jesus' name.

- Anything that has been stolen from me I take back by fire, in the name of Jesus.

PRAYER TO RECEIVE DIVINE FAVOR

By Dr. Stella Immanuel

Divine favor makes the difference in our everyday lives. If the Lord starts favoring you, many things in your life will be easy. Favor has already been released from heaven to us as children of God, but we have to appropriate it. The Word of God does not come void, so as we start praying and decreeing the word of favor, favor will pursue us and overtake us, in Jesus' name.

Favor is a key that opens doors. Even great doors swing open on just three or four hinges. Your opportunities are hinged to just a few key relationships. I've heard it said that it's not necessary for everyone to like you, just the right people.

> But the LORD was with Joseph, and shewed him mercy, and gave him favor in the sight of the keeper of the prison.
>
> —GENESIS 39:21

> And the LORD gave the people favor in the sight of the Egyptians. Moreover the man Moses was very great in the land of Egypt, in the sight of Pharaoh's servants, and in the sight of the people.
>
> —EXODUS 11:3

> And of Naphtali he said, O Naphtali, satisfied with favor, and full with the blessing of the LORD: possess thou the west and the south.
>
> —DEUTERONOMY 33:23

> For thou, LORD, wilt bless the righteous; with favor wilt thou compass him as with a shield.
>
> —PSALM 5:12

> And Jesus increased in wisdom and stature, and in favor with God and man.
>
> —LUKE 2:52

> And the child Samuel grew on, and was in favor both with the Lord, and also with men.
>
> —1 SAMUEL 2:26

> And it was so, when the king saw Esther the queen standing in the court, that she obtained favour in his sight: and the king held out to Esther the golden sceptre that was in his

hand. So Esther drew near, and touched the top of the sceptre.

—Esther 5:2

Prayer Points

- O God, arise and show me mercy and favor in ministry, business, marriage, and so on, in Jesus' name.

- As you clothed the children of Israel with favor in Egypt, clothe me with favor so heathens can bless me, in the name of Jesus.

- Give me favor in the sight of men. Give my ministry favor in the sight of men, and give my business favor in the sight of customers, in Jesus' name.

- Satisfy me, Lord, with favor, and fill me with blessings, in the name of Jesus.

- I receive favor with God and with man in everything I do, in the name of Jesus.

- My Father, give me favor with kings and great men of this world, in Jesus' name.

- O God, arise and encompass me with favor as with a shield, in the name of Jesus.

Prayer to Release What the Enemy Has Swallowed

By Dr. Stella Immanuel

Many children of God are wallowing in poverty and lack even though the Word says we are blessed in the city and in the fields. God has given us everything pertaining to life and godliness. So if there is a general absence of the blessing of God, we need to do something about it. Our blessing has been swallowed up. We need to pray with holy violence until our riches are vomited by the enemy and we are living in the blessing of God.

> He hath swallowed down riches, and he shall vomit them up again: God shall cast them out of his belly.
>
> —Job 20:15

> That which he laboured for shall he restore, and shall not swallow it down: according to his substance shall the restitution be, and he shall not rejoice therein.
>
> —Job 20:18

> Men do not despise a thief, if he steals to satisfy his soul when he is hungry; but if he be found, he shall restore sevenfold; he shall give all the substance of his house.
>
> —Proverbs 6:30–31

> In that day the Lord with his sore and great and strong sword shall punish leviathan the piercing serpent, even leviathan that crooked serpent; and he shall slay the dragon that is in the sea.
>
> —Isaiah 27:1

Prayer Points

- Father, forgive me for all my sins (list them), and cleanse me from all unrighteousness.

- O God, arise and make me Your battle-ax and a sharp threshing instrument, in the name of Jesus.

- O God, arise and cut the head of every serpent, every dragon that has swallowed my blessing with the sword of fire, in Jesus' name.

- I cut open, I burst open, I tear open the belly of the serpent and the dragon, and I release my stuff, in Jesus' name.

- I command every serpent and dragon to vomit everything you have swallowed—my riches, my marriage, my ministry, my virtue, my children. Vomit them by fire, vomit them by fire, vomit them by fire, in Jesus' name.

- O God, arise, cast my virtue, my ministry, my money, and so on, out of the belly of the dragon, the serpent, the earth, the grave, the water, in the name of Jesus. Cast them out, cast them out, cast them out, in Jesus' name.

- I command sevenfold restoration of everything the enemy has swallowed—my money, my children, my virtue, my marriage, in Jesus' name.

- You, my blessings, my money, my favor, my marriage in the heavenlies, the earth, the water, in the forest and satanic banks—locate me by fire, in the name of Jesus. Locate me by fire, locate me by fire, locate me by fire, in Jesus' name.

PRAYER TO RECEIVE MIRACLE-WORKING POWER

By Dr. Stella Immanuel

John answered their questions by saying, "I baptize with water; but someone is coming soon who is greater than I am—so much greater that I am not even worthy to be his slave....He will baptize you with the Holy Spirit and with fire."

—LUKE 3:16, NLT

And of the angels he saith, Who maketh his angels spirits, and his ministers a flame of fire.

—HEBREWS 1:7

That confirmeth the word of his servant, and performeth the counsel of his messengers

—ISAIAH 44:26

And he said unto them, Go ye into all the world, and preach the gospel to every creature. He that believeth and is baptized shall be saved; but he that believeth not shall be damned. And these signs shall follow them that believe; in my name shall they cast out devils; they shall speak with new tongues; they shall take up serpents; and if they drink any deadly thing, it shall not hurt them; they shall lay hands on the sick, and they shall recover.

—MARK 16:15–18

Verily, verily, I say unto you, Except a corn of wheat fall into the ground and die, it abideth alone: but if it die, it bringeth forth much fruit.

—JOHN 12:24

And, behold, I send the promise of my Father upon you: but tarry ye in the city of Jerusalem, until ye be endued with power from on high.

—LUKE 24:49

PRAYER POINTS

- O God, arise and pour out the Spirit of grace and supplication on me, in the name of Jesus.

- O God, arise and baptize me with the Holy Ghost and fire, in the name of Jesus.

- You make Your ministers flames of fire. Make me a flame of fire, O Lord, in the name of Jesus.

- Breath of heaven, breathe on me. Wind of God, blow on me and endow me with miracle-working power, in Jesus' name.

- Power to do exploits for the kingdom, power that cannot be challenged by the kingdom of darkness, fall upon me in the name of Jesus.

- As Your messenger, O Lord, confirm the words I decree and back my word with miracles, signs, and wonders, in Jesus' name.

- My Father, my God, as I tarry in Your presence, break me, remold me, and endow me with power from on high, in the name of Jesus.

PRAYERS TO KILL THE MARRIAGE KILLERS
By Rev. Dr. Mosy and Rev. Mrs. Gloria Madugba

Whoso findeth a wife findeth a good thing, and obtaineth favour of the LORD.

—PROVERBS 18:22

And said, For this cause shall a man leave father and mother, and shall cleave to his wife: and they twain shall be one flesh? Wherefore they are no more twain, but one flesh. What therefore God hath joined together, let not man put asunder.

—MATTHEW 19:5–6

If the foundations be destroyed, what can the righteous do?

—PSALM 11:3

Thy wife shall be as a fruitful vine by the sides of thine house: thy children like olive plants round about thy table.

—PSALM 128:3

Let thy fountain be blessed: and rejoice with the wife of thy youth.

—PROVERBS 5:18

House and riches are the inheritance of fathers and a prudent wife is from the Lord.

—PROVERBS 19:14

Who can find a virtuous woman? for her price is far above rubies.

—PROVERBS 31:10

Two are better than one; because they have a good reward for their labour.

—ECCLESIASTES 4:9

Again, if two lie together, then they have heat: but how can one be warm alone? And if one prevail against him, two shall withstand him; and a threefold cord is not quickly broken.

—ECCLESIASTES 4:11–12

How should one chase a thousand, and two put ten thousand to flight, except their Rock had sold them, and the LORD had shut them up?

—DEUTERONOMY 32:30

And the Lord God said, It is not good that the man should be alone; I will make him an help meet for him. Therefore shall a man leave his father and his mother, and shall cleave unto his wife: and they shall be one flesh. And they were both naked, the man and his wife, and were not ashamed.

—Genesis 2:18, 24–25

Yet ye say, Wherefore? Because the Lord hath been witness between thee and the wife of thy youth, against whom thou hast dealt treacherously: yet is she thy companion, and the wife of thy covenant. And did not he make one? Yet had he the residue of the spirit. And wherefore one? That he might seek a godly seed. Therefore take heed to your spirit, and let none deal treacherously against the wife of his youth. For the Lord, the God of Israel, saith that he hateth putting away: for one covereth violence with his garment, saith the Lord of hosts: therefore take heed to your spirit, that ye deal not treacherously.

—Malachi 2:14–16

Prayer Points

- Lord, open my eyes to know Your plans and purposes for instituting my marriage on earth.

- Let every evil stronghold of the enemy that is stopping my marriage from fulfilling her destiny be dismantled.

- Lord, make my marriage a blessing and an instrument for You, in Jesus' name.

- Let every evil foundation speaking against my marriage be destroyed, in Jesus' name.

- Lord, give me the wisdom, ability, and commitment to take adequate care of this precious gift of marriage You gave to me.

- I call forth every enablement from God that my marriage needs to impact my generation. Lord, open my eyes to see any of the joy killers that exist in my marriage.

- I command these joy killers to die in my marriage.

- I secure my marriage with the blood of Jesus Christ, that it will be impossible for any of these joy killers to spring up and flourish in it.

- I call forth a full restoration of every joy that has been killed by these joy killers.

- Lord, make my husband/wife sensitive to the things that eat up my joy in our marriage, and help him/her to avoid them.

- Lord, give me a revelation of my marriage the way You see it.

- Open my eyes to these things that are eating up my marital joy, whether they are mentioned in this chapter or not.

- I speak death to these joy killers in my marriage in Jesus' name.

- I frustrate and come against the strategies of the devil to steal my joy in my marriage.

- I soak my marriage in the blood of Jesus Christ and declare that these joy killers will not flourish in it, in Jesus' name.

- Let the blood of Jesus speak over my marriage and silence every evil speaking from our foundations.

- Let every root of pride in our lives be destroyed.

- Lord, give us a second touch that will deal with every flesh manifesting in our marriage.

- Lord, open our eyes to every doorway and loophole in our lives through which the enemy attacks our marriage.

- We refuse to fight each other in our marriage but will join forces together to fight the devil and the stubborn pursuers eating up our marital joy.

- We revoke every evil decree, evil covenants, curses, or manipulations from hell affecting our marriage.

- Let all the joy killers troubling our marriage die in Jesus' name.

- Lord, I receive supernatural strength and enablement to kill the killers of my marital joy.

- Lord, deliver me from being overcome by evil. Teach me how to overcome evil with good in my marriage.

- Lord, open my eyes to see Your rich deposits and potentials in my husband/wife, and teach me to appreciate and maximize them.

- Lord, help me to see the real me, with all my shortcomings. Give me grace to see where I am failing You and destroying my marriage. Help me to be willing to amend my ways, in Jesus' name.

- Lord, make me a wise woman who builds her home, or make me an exemplary leader and priest over my home, in Jesus' name.

- Lord, encounter me so that the beauty of Jesus will be seen in my life and in my marriage.

- Lord, transform me and use me to bring about a major transformation in my marriage, in Jesus' name.

- Lord, open my eyes to the areas where I have missed it. Help me make the needed sacrifices to recover my husband/wife and my marriage.

- Lord, help us see our marriage through Your eyes and be willing to allow it to become what You originally intended for it.

- Make us instruments in Your hands to kill the killers of marriage both in ours and other marriages.

- Lord, make our marriage a showcase to our generation of Your original intent for marriages.

- We call forth all that pertains to life and godliness from Your throne to enable us to fulfill Your mandate on earth for our marriages.

- We pursue in unity all the stubborn pursuers of our marriage and speak death to them, in Jesus' name.

- We command every satanic padlock holding our marriage to be roasted by fire, in Jesus' name.

- Let every blessing God has packaged for our marriages locate us, in Jesus' name.

- Lord, heal every aspect of our marriages and rekindle the flame that made us one in Jesus. Lord, make our children sources of joy, encouragement, and blessings to our marriage.

- Lord, teach them all that pertains to life and godliness, in Jesus' name.

- Lord, make our children godly and sample seeds that will impact their generation and fulfill their destiny.

- Lord, give us the wisdom to raise them up in Your fear and to carry them along as major parts of our lives and ministry.

- Lord, make our sons cornerstones and fashion our daughters after the similitude of a place, in Jesus' name.

- Lord, encounter our children and bring them into a personal relationship with You. We robe them into a covenant relationship with You that cannot be broken.

- We command the star-hunters who want to stop them from fulfilling their destinies to be destroyed, in Jesus' name.

- Lord, we repent for every way we have not done well in the area of fellowship in our marriage.

- We destroy every rock in our mattress that is affecting our fellowship and making it unhealthy.

- We receive a new revelation in this aspect of our marriage that will help us to get the best from it.

- Lord, please heal our fellowship and pour a new wine into it that will rekindle our marriage, in Jesus' name.

- We receive Your grace to excel in our fellowship and in every other aspect of our marriage, in Jesus' name.

PRAYERS FOR THE NATION
From the Works of Dr. D. K. Olukoya

I exhort therefore, that, first of all, supplications, prayers, intercessions, and giving of thanks, be made for all men; for kings, and for all that are in authority; that we may lead a quiet and peaceable life in all godliness and honesty.

—1 TIMOTHY 2:1–2

See, I have this day set thee over the nations and over the kingdoms, to root out, and to pull down, and to destroy, and to throw down, to build, and to plant.

—JEREMIAH 1:10

The Spirit of the Lord God is upon me; because the LORD hath anointed me to preach good tidings unto the meek; he hath sent me to bind up the brokenhearted, to proclaim liberty to the captives, and the opening of the prison to them that are bound; to proclaim the acceptable year of the Lord, and the day of vengeance of our God; to comfort all that mourn; to appoint unto them that mourn in Zion, to give unto them beauty for ashes, the oil of joy for mourning, the garment of praise for the spirit of heaviness; that they might be called trees of righteousness, the planting of the Lord, that he might be glorified. And they shall build the old wastes, they shall raise up the former desolations, and they shall repair the waste cities, the desolations of many generations. And strangers shall stand and feed your flocks, and the sons of the alien shall be your plowmen and your vinedressers. But ye shall be named the Priests of the LORD: men shall call you the Ministers of our God: ye shall eat the riches of the Gentiles, and in their glory shall ye boast yourselves.

—ISAIAH 61:1-6

Finally, my brethren, be strong in the Lord, and in the power of his might. Put on the whole armour of God, that ye may be able to stand against the wiles of the devil. For we wrestle not against flesh and blood, but against principalities, against powers, against the rulers of the darkness of this world, against spiritual wickedness in high places. Wherefore take unto you the whole armour of God, that ye may be able to withstand in the evil day, and having done all, to stand. Stand therefore, having your loins girt about with truth, and having on the breastplate of righteousness; and your feet shod with the preparation of the gospel of peace; above all, taking the shield of faith, wherewith ye shall be able to quench all the fiery darts of the wicked.

—EPHESIANS 6:10–16

PRAYER POINTS

Father, in the name of Jesus, we confess all the sins and iniquities of the land, of our ancestors, of our leaders, and of the people, including violence, rejection of God, corruption, idolatries, robbery, suspicion, injustice, bitterness, bloody riots, pogroms, rebellion, conspiracy, the shedding of innocent blood, tribal conflicts, child kidnapping and murder, occultism, mismanagement, negligence, and more.

- We plead for mercy and forgiveness in the name of Jesus.

- O Lord, remember our land and redeem our land.

- O Lord, save our land from destruction and judgment.

- Let Your healing power begin to operate upon our land, in the name of Jesus.

- Let all forces of darkness hindering the move of God in this nation be rendered impotent, in the name of Jesus.

- We command the spiritual strongman in charge of this country to be bound and disgraced, in the name of Jesus.

- Let every evil establishment and satanic tree in this country be uprooted and cast into fire, in the name of Jesus.

- We come against every spirit of the antichrist working against this nation, and we command them to be permanently frustrated, in the name of Jesus.

- We command the stones of fire from God to fall upon every national satanic operation and activity, in Jesus' name.

- Let the desire, plans, devices, and expectations of the enemy for this country be completely frustrated, in Jesus' name.

- Let every satanic curse on this nation fall down to the ground and die, in the name of Jesus.

- By the blood of Jesus, let all sins, ungodliness, idolatry, and all vices cease in the land, in the name of Jesus.

- We break every evil covenant and dedication made upon our land, in the name of Jesus.

- We plead the blood of Jesus over the nation, in Jesus' name.

- We decree the will of God for this land, whether the devil likes it or not, in the name of Jesus.

- Let all contrary powers and authorities in this nation be confounded and put to shame, in the name of Jesus.

- We close every satanic gate in every city of this country, in Jesus' name.

- Let every evil throne in this country be dashed to pieces, in Jesus' name.

- We bind all negative forces operating in the lives of our leaders in this country, in the name of Jesus.

- O Lord, lay Your hands of fire and power upon all our leaders in this country, in the name of Jesus.

- We bind every blood-drinking demon in this country, in Jesus' name.

- Let the Prince of Peace reign in every department of this nation, in the name of Jesus.

- Let every anti-gospel spirit be frustrated and rendered impotent, in the name of Jesus.

- O Lord, give us leaders in this country who will see their roles as a calling instead of an opportunity to amass wealth.

- Let all forms of ungodliness be destroyed by the divine fire of burning, in the name of Jesus.

- O Lord, let our leaders in this country be filled with divine understanding and wisdom.

- O Lord, let our leaders in this country follow the counsel of God and not of man and demons.

- O Lord, let our leaders in this country have wisdom and knowledge of God.

- O Lord, let our government be the kind that would obtain direction and leading of God.

- Let every satanic altar in this country receive the fire of God and be burned to ashes, in the name of Jesus.

- We silence every satanic prophet, priest, and practitioner, in the mighty name of Jesus. We forbid them from interfering with the affairs of this nation, in the name of Jesus.

- Let the blood of Jesus cleanse our land from every blood pollution, in the name of Jesus.

- We command the fire of God on all idols, sacrifices, rituals, shrines, and local satanic thrones in this country, in Jesus' name.

- We break any conscious and unconscious agreement made between the people of this country and Satan, in Jesus' name.

- We dedicate and claim all our cities for Jesus, in Jesus' name.

- Let the blessings and presence of the Lord be experienced in all our cities, in the name of Jesus.

- We decree total paralysis on lawlessness, immorality, and drug addiction in this country, in the name of Jesus.

- Let the power, love, and glory of God be established in our land, in the name of Jesus.

- Let there be a thirst and hunger for God in the hearts of Christians of this nation, in the name of Jesus.

- O Lord, deposit the spirit of revival in this nation.

- O Lord, lay Your hands of power and might upon the armed forces and police, establishments and institutions, universities and colleges of this country.

- Let the resurrection power of the Lord Jesus Christ fall upon our economy in this country, in the name of Jesus.

- Let there be fruitfulness and prosperity in every area of this country, in the name of Jesus.

- We command every threat to the political, economic, and social stability in the land to be paralyzed, in the name of Jesus.

- We frustrate every satanic external influence by other nations, in the name of Jesus.

- We command confusion and disagreement between the sons of the bondwoman planning to cage the nation, in Jesus' name.

- We break any covenant between any satanic external influence and our leaders, in the name of Jesus.

- We paralyze every spirit of wastage of economic resources in this country, in the name of Jesus.

- Let the spirit of borrowing depart completely from this country, in the name of Jesus.

- O Lord, show Yourself mighty in the affairs of this nation.

- Let the kingdom of Christ reign in this nation, in Jesus' name.

- O Lord, do new things in our country to show Your power and greatness to the heathen.

- Let the kingdom of our Lord Jesus Christ come into the heart of every person in this country, in the name of Jesus.

- O Lord, have mercy upon this nation.

- Let all the glory of this nation that has departed be restored, in the name of Jesus.

- Let all un-evangelized areas of this country be reached with the gospel of our Lord Jesus Christ, in the name of Jesus.

- O Lord, send forth laborers into Your vineyard to reach the unreached in this country.

- We dismantle the stronghold of poverty in this nation, in Jesus' name.

- O Lord, install Your agenda for this nation. Let every power of darkness operating in our educational institutions be disgraced, in the name of Jesus.

- Let the satanic representatives of key posts in this country be dismantled, in the name of Jesus.

- Let every evil spiritual throne behind all physical thrones in this nation be dismantled, in the name of Jesus.

- Let every satanic covenant made on behalf of this country by anyone be nullified, in the name of Jesus.

- We trample upon the serpents and scorpions of ethnic clashes in this country, in the name of Jesus.

- We decree a realignment of the situation around us to favor us in this country, in the name of Jesus.

- We dethrone every strange king installed in the spirit upon us in this country, in the name of Jesus.

- Let all principalities, powers, rulers of darkness, and spiritual wickedness in heavenly places militating against this nation be bound and disgraced, in the name of Jesus.

- Let righteousness reign in every part of this nation, in Jesus' name.

Thank you for joining me in declaring and believing these powerful prayer points. Let the Word of God ever be in our mouths, and there is no way we can lose any battle. Rather, we will be the battle-axes of God, overcoming every obstacle, achieving victory over every adversary, and emerging more glorious than ever before—as individuals, families, churches, cities, and nations.

Let the people of God arise—and let America live!

MY COVID–19 PROTECTIVE MEASURES AND TREATMENT PROTOCOLS

O F THE MORE than seven thousand COVID-infected or symptomatic patients I have treated at my Houston clinic and via telemedicine, I have lost only eight precious souls. Around the world more than sixteen thousand people have come to my website, drstellamd.com, and benefited from the prophylaxis protocols I have shared with them. I include my treatment protocols and protective measures here for information purposes. I have seen thousands of patients respond well to these protocols. However, everyone's health is unique, and you should not make any changes to your medication or diet without first consulting a medical professional who is aware of your unique health profile.

PROTECTIVE MEASURES

As a protective measure, I generally recommend patients follow one of these two regimens:

Hydroxychloroquine regimen

- 200 mg tablets—one tablet weekly if 180 pounds or less; two tablets weekly if over 180 pounds
- vitamin C—1,000 mg once daily
- vitamin D$_3$—2,000 IUs once daily
- zinc—30 mg once daily
- N-acetyl cysteine (NAC)—600 mg twice daily

Ivermectin regimen

- 3 mg tablets—four tablets weekly if 200 pounds or less; six tablets weekly if over 200 pounds
- vitamin C—1,000 mg once daily
- vitamin D$_3$—2,000 IUs once daily
- zinc—30 mg once daily
- N-acetyl cysteine (NAC)—600 mg twice daily

Treatment Protocol if Exposed

The following is what I have recommended to patients who were exposed to COVID-19 and have no symptoms. Patients would follow one of these two regimens:

Hydroxychloroquine regimen

- 200 mg tablets—two tablets on day 1; one tablet on days 2 through 5; then one tablet weekly if 180 pounds or less, or two tablets weekly if over 180 pounds
- vitamin C—1,000 mg once daily

- vitamin D$_3$—2,000 IUs once daily
- zinc—30 mg once daily
- N-acetyl cysteine (NAC)—600 mg twice daily

Ivermectin regimen

- 3 mg tablets—if 200 pounds or less, take four tablets each on days 1, 3, and 5, and then take four tablets once a week; if over 200 pounds, take six tablets each on days 1, 3, and 5, and then take six tablets weekly
- vitamin C—1,000 mg once daily
- vitamin D$_3$—2,000 IUs once daily
- zinc—30 mg once daily
- N-acetyl cysteine (NAC)—600 mg twice daily

TREATMENT PROTOCOL IF SICK

Again, this cannot replace consultation with a doctor who knows your unique health profile, but I have seen thousands of patients who were sick with COVID-19 respond well to the following treatment protocol—which includes both hydroxychloroquine and ivermectin:

- hydroxychloroquine—200 mg tablets
  - » If 180 pounds or less, two tablets twice on day 1; then one tablet twice daily on days 2 through 5; then one tablet weekly

» If over 180 pounds, two tablets twice on day 1;
then one tablet twice daily on days 2 through 5;
then two tablets weekly

- ivermectin—3 mg tablets

  » if 130 to 200 pounds, four tablets daily for five
  days
  » if 201 to 250 pounds, six tablets daily for five
  days
  » if 251 to 350 pounds, eight tablets daily for five
  days
  » if over 350 pounds, ten tablets daily for five days

- doxycycline—100 mg twice daily for ten days

- prednisone—two 20 mg tablets by mouth daily
  for five days (if not diabetic)

- budesonide nebulizer solution—one 0.5 mg vial
  daily for seven days

- albuterol nebulizer solution—one 2.5 mg/3mL
  vial as needed every six hours (I prescribe one
  box, no refills.)

- brompheniramine, dextromethorphan, and pseu-
  doephedrine (An example is Bromfed DM.)—one
  to two teaspoons by mouth daily as needed for
  cough (I prescribe 8 ounces with no refills.)

- promethazine—one 25 mg tablet by mouth as
  needed every six hours for nausea (I prescribe
  twenty tablets with no refills.)

- loperamide—one 2 mg tablet by mouth daily as needed for loose stools (I prescribe twenty tablets with no refills.)

- baby aspirin—one 81 mg tablet daily (I prescribe thirty tablets.)

- electrolyte drink such as Pedialyte—two liters a day

- vitamins—vitamin C: 1,000 mg once daily; vitamin D_3: 2,000 IUs once daily; zinc: 30 mg once daily; N-acetyl cysteine (NAC)—600 mg twice daily

ADDITIONAL CLINICAL WISDOM

- Stay hydrated.

- Use incentive spirometer to expand your lungs.

- Put lemongrass in hot water and inhale.

NOTES

CHAPTER 1

1. "We Have Been Lied To—American Doctors Address COVID-19 Misinformation at Scotus Press Conference," BitChute, July 28, 2020, https://www.bitchute.com/video/zr04GsUupOwk/.
2. "Medicines for the Prevention of Malaria While Traveling Hydroxychloroquine (Plaquenil™)," Centers for Disease Control and Prevention, accessed June 28, 2021, https://www.cdc.gov/malaria/resources/pdf/fsp/drugs/hydroxychloroquine.pdf; Nicola Principi and Susanna Esposito, "Chloroquine or Hydroxychloroquine for Prophylaxis of COVID-19," *The Lancet* 20, no. 10 (October 1, 2020): P1118, https://doi.org/10.1016/S1473-3099(20)30296-6.

CHAPTER 4

1. Stella Immanuel, "In 2012 the Lord showed me in a vision of the night that something terrible was going to happen in the US to change the world as we know it," Facebook, January 12, 2016, 4:47 a.m., https://www.facebook.com/drstella.gwp/posts/10154008814914180.
2. Stella Immanuel, "Last night I was asking the Lord for details and what must be done," Facebook, January 13, 2016, 2:34 a.m., https://www.facebook.com/drstella.gwp/posts/10154011375774180.

CHAPTER 5

1. News.com.au, "Coronavirus: Disturbing footage shows truck 'loading bodies' outside New York hospital," YouTube, March 30, 2020, https://www.youtube.com/watch?v=SxguV0KXbEc.
2. Bernard Condon and Jennifer Peltz, "AP: Over 9,000 Virus Patients Sent Into NY Nursing Homes," Associated Press, February 11, 2021, https://apnews.com/article/new-york-andrew-cuomo-us-news-coronavirus-pandemic-nursing-homes-512cae0abb55a55f375b3192f2cdd6b5.
3. Minyvonne Burke, Suzanne Ciechalski, and Dawn Liu, "Video Appears to Show People in China Forcibly Taken for Quarantine Over Coronavirus," NBC News, February 8, 2020, https://www.nbcnews.com/news/world/video-appears-show-people-china-forcibly-taken-quarantine-over-coronavirus-n1133096; Agence France-Presse, "A Man Lies Dead in the Street: the Image That Captures the Wuhan Coronavirus Crisis," *The Guardian*, January 30, 2020, https://www.theguardian.com/world/2020/jan/31/a-man-lies-dead-in-the-street-the-image-that-captures-the-wuhan-coronavirus-crisis.
4. Menggiang Luo et al., "Intubation, Mortality, and Risk Factors in Critically Ill COVID-19 Patients: A Pilot Study," *Journal of Clinical*

Anesthesia 67 (2020): 110039, https://dx.doi.org/10.1016%2Fj. jclinane.2020.110039; Safiya Richardson et al., "Presenting Characteristics, Comorbidities, and Outcomes Among 5700 Patients Hospitalized With COVID-19 in the New York City Area," *Journal of the American Medical Association* 323, no. 20 (2020): 2052–2059, https://doi.org/10.1001/jama.2020.6775.

5. Courtney Brogle, "Hospital Incorrectly Declared COVID-19 Patient Dead Twice, Family Claims," *Newsweek*, April 20, 2021, https://www.newsweek.com/hospital-incorrectly-declared-covid-19-patient-dead-twice-family-claims-1585163; Taylor Coleman, "Former Miss Virginia Comes Back to Life After Being Declared Dead From COVID-19," ABC 13 News, December 30, 2020, https://wset.com/news/local/former-miss-virginia-comes-back-to-life-after-doctors-declare-her-dead-from-covid-19; Joshua Rhett Miller, "Stricken Coronavirus Nurse: 'Gross Negligence' Has Patients Dying at NYC Hospitals," *New York Post*, May 5, 2020, https://nypost.com/2020/05/05/coronavirus-nurse-says-negligence-has-patients-dying-at-nyc-hospitals/; Olivier1985, "Nicole Sirotek," YouTube, May 4, 2020, https://www.youtube.com/watch?v=CvhTQV5FNUE.

6. Christian News 360, "COVID-19 Briefing: Current Quarantine Approach Wrong Based on Science | Dr Erickson & Dr Massihi Pt1," YouTube, April 24, 2020, https://web.archive.org/web/20200428040832if_/https://www.youtube.com/watch?v=vJprwe_rWeM.

7. Lizandra Portal, "Man Who Died in Motorcycle Crash Counted as COVID-19 Death in Florida: Report," CBS 12 News, July 18, 2020, https://cbs12.com/news/local/man-who-died-in-motorcycle-crash-counted-as-covid-19-death-in-florida-report; "Colorado Coroner Calling Out How State Classifies COVID-19 Deaths," KMOV4, December 18, 2020, https://www.kmov.com/news/colorado-coroner-calling-out-how-state-classifies-covid-19-deaths/article_297e3550-4131-11eb-9f01-ffe3e11d0f46.html; Iowa's News Now Staff, "CR Man Mistakenly Listed in New York Times' Front-Page COVID-19 Obituaries," *Iowa News Now*, May 24, 2020, https://cbs2iowa.com/news/local/cr-man-mistakenly-listed-in-new-york-times-front-page-covid-19-obituaries.

8. Neeraj Sinha and Galit Balayla, "Hydroxychloroquine and COVID-19," *Postgrad Medical Journal* 96 (April 15, 2020): 550–555, https://doi.org/10.1136/postgradmedj-2020-137785; Jia Liu et al., "Hydroxychloroquine, a Less Toxic Derivative of Chloroquine, Is Effective in Inhibiting SARS-CoV-2 Infection in Vitro," *Cell Discovery* 6, no. 16 (March 18, 2020), https://doi.org/10.1038/s41421-020-0156-0; Philippe Colson et al., "Chloroquine and Hydroxychloroquine as Available Weapons to Fight COVID-19," *International Journal of Antimicrobial*

Agents 5, no. 41 (March 14, 2020), https://covid-19.conacyt.mx/jspui/bitstream/1000/1107/1/105581.pdf.

9. Martin J. Vincent et al., "Chloroquine Is a Potent Inhibitor of SARS Coronavirus Infection and Spread," *Virology Journal* 2, no. 69 (2005), https://doi.org/10.1186/1743-422X-2-69.

10. Jean-Christophe Lagier et al., "Outcomes of 3,737 COVID-19 Patients Treated With Hydroxychloroquine/Azithromycin and Other Regimens in Marseille, France: A Retrospective Analysis," *Journal of Travel Medicine and Infectious Disease* 36 (July–August 2020): 101791, https://doi.org/10.1016/j.tmaid.2020.101791; Philippe Gautret et al., "Response to the Use of Hydroxychloroquine in Combination With Azithromycin for Patients With COVID-19 Is Not Supported by Recent Literature," *International Journal of Antimicrobial Agents* 57, no. 1 (January 2021): 106241, https://doi.org/10.1016/j.ijantimicag.2020.106241; Roland Derwand, Martin Scholz, and Vladimir Zelenko, "COVID-19 Outpatients: Early Risk-Stratified Treatment With Zinc Plus Low-Dose Hydroxychloroquine and Azithromycin: A Retrospective Case Series Study," *International Journal of Antimicrobial Agents* 56, no. 6 (December 2020): 106214, https://doi.org/10.1016/j.ijantimicag.2020.106214. The preprint of this article was available online July 3, 2020.

11. Martin J. Vincent, Eric Bergeron, Suzanne Benjannet, Bobbie R. Erickson, Pierre E. Rollin, Thomas G. Ksiazek, Nabil G. Seidah, and Stuart T. Nichol, "Chloroquine Is a Potent Inhibitor of SARS Coronavirus Infection and Spread," *Virology Journal*, August 22, 2005, doi: 10.1186/1743-422X-2-69.

12. "Coronavirus: Hydroxychloroquine Ineffective Says Fauci," BBC News, July 29, 2020, https://www.bbc.com/news/world-us-canada-53575964.

13. "Medicines for the Prevention of Malaria While Traveling Hydroxychloroquine (Plaquenil™)," Centers for Disease Control and Prevention.

14. "Hydroxychloroquine," MedlinePlus, accessed June 30, 2021, https://medlineplus.gov/druginfo/meds/a601240.html; cf. "Hydroxychloroquine," MedlinePlus, archived April 21, 2020, https://web.archive.org/web/20200421053250/https://medlineplus.gov/druginfo/meds/a601240.html. See also "Hydroxychloroquine," Drugs.com, accessed June 30, 2021, https://www.drugs.com/hydroxychloroquine.html; cf. "Hydroxychloroquine," Drugs.com, archived April 10, 2020, https://web.archive.org/web/20200410160738/https://www.drugs.com/hydroxychloroquine.html.

15. Jamie L. Thompson and Ryan R. Crossman, "Drug-Induced QT Prolongation," *US Pharmacist*, February 20, 2007, https://www.

uspharmacist.com/article/drug-induced-qt-prolongation; Rohan Jayasinghe and Pramesh Kovoor, "Drugs and the QTc Interval," *Australian Prescriber* 25 (May 1, 2002): 63–65, https://doi.org/10.18773/austprescr.2002.058; BC Inherited Arrhythmia Program, "List of Drugs to be Avoided by Patients With Congenital Long QT Syndrome (LQTS)," Heart Centre, updated February 2017, https://www.heartcentre.ca/sites/default/files/Long%20QT%20Drugs%20-%20Feb%2022%202017%20_alternatives_.pdf.

16. "Bactrim," Food and Drug Administration, updated June 13, 2013, https://www.accessdata.fda.gov/drugsatfda_docs/label/2013/017377s068s073lbl.pdf.

17. "FDA Drug Safety Communication: Azithromycin (Zithromax or Zmax) and the Risk of Potentially Fatal Heart Rhythms," Food and Drug Administration, March 12, 2013, https://www.fda.gov/files/drugs/published/FDA-Drug-Safety-Communication--Azithromycin-%28Zithromax-or-Zmax%29-and-the-risk-of-potentially-fatal-heart-rhythms-%28view-and-print-version%29.pdf.

18. "CIPRO (Ciprofloxacin Hydrochloride): Highlights of Prescribing Information," Food and Drug Administration, updated July 2016, https://www.accessdata.fda.gov/drugsatfda_docs/label/2016/019537s086lbl.pdf.

19. "Patients Need Ability to Choose Hydroxychloroquine, States AAPS," Association of American Physicians and Surgeons, news release, May 28, 2020, https://aapsonline.org/patients-need-ability-to-choose-hydroxychloroquine-states-aaps/.

20. "Hydroxychloroquine (Plaquenil): Benefits, Side Effects, and Dosing," National Resource Center on Lupus, accessed June 30, 2021, https://www.lupus.org/resources/drug-spotlight-on-hydroxychloroquine; "Hydroxychloroquine (Plaquenil®) Drug Information Sheet," Johns Hopkins Arthritis Center, accessed June 30, 2021, https://www.hopkinsarthritis.org/patient-corner/drug-information/hydroxychloroquine-plaquenil/.

21. "Dr. Gupta Explains Concerns Over Medicines Touted by Trump," CNN, April 9, 2020, https://www.cnn.com/videos/health/2020/04/09/hydroxychloroquine-zinc-medicines-coronavirus-donald-trump-gupta-cpt-vpx.cnn.

22. Associated Press, "'Anecdotal Evidence,' Dr. Fauci Says of Malaria Drug Claim," *New York Times*, March 20, 2020, https://www.nytimes.com/video/us/politics/100000007046134/trump-fauci.html.

23. Patrick Hanks, ed., Dictionary of American Family Names, s.v. "Fauci," (Oxford, UK: Oxford University Press, 2003), 555, https://www.

google.com/books/edition/Dictionary_of_American_Family_Names/
FJoDDAAAQBAJ?hl=en&gbpv=0.

24. Kathleen Gray, "Trump Singles Out Detroit Democrat for Praise
    Because She Took His Advice," *USA Today*, updated April 8, 2020,
    https://www.usatoday.com/story/news/local/michigan/2020/04/07/
    trump-praises-detroit-democrat-karen-whitsett/2966482001/; Sarah
    Rahal and Beth LeBlanc, "Detroit Democrats Unanimously Censure
    Lawmaker Who Credited Trump for COVID-19 Recovery," *Detroit
    News*, updated April 25, 2020, https://www.detroitnews.com/story/
    news/local/detroit-city/2020/04/25/detroit-democrats-unanimously-
    censure-lawmaker-karen-whitsett-who-credited-trump-covid-19-
    recovery/3025907001/.

25. Joseph Magagnoli et al., "Outcomes of Hydroxychloroquine
    Usage in United States Veterans Hospitalized With COVID-
    19," *medRvix*, preprint (April 23, 2020), https://dx.doi.org/10.110
    1%2F2020.04.16.20065920.

26. Robert L. Wilkie, letter to Veteran Service Organization Partners, April
    29, 2020, https://www.airforcemag.com/app/uploads/2020/04/VSO-
    Letter-4-29-2020.pdf.

27. "Dr. Gupta Explains Concerns Over Medicines Touted by Trump," CNN.

28. Phil McCausland and Jonathan Allen, "Veterans Affairs Has Provided
    Few Answers Around Coronavirus Study, Advocates Say," NBC,
    updated April 26, 2020, https://www.nbcnews.com/news/us-news/
    veteran-advocates-say-va-has-provided-few-answers-around-
    agency-n1190791.

29. Mandeep R. Mehra et al., "Retracted: Hydroxychloroquine or
    Chloroquine With or Without a Macrolide for Treatment of COVID-
    19: A Multinational Registry Analysis," *The Lancet*, May 22, 2020,
    https://doi.org/10.1016/S0140-6736(20)31180-6.

30. Jason Beaubien, "WHO Halts Hydroxychloroquine Trial Over
    Safety Concerns," NPR, May 25, 2020, https://www.npr.org/
    sections/coronavirus-live-updates/2020/05/25/861913688/who-halts-
    hydroxychloroquine-trial-over-safety-concerns.

31. Elizabeth Cohen, "Yet Another Study Shows Hydroxychloroquine
    Doesn't Work Against COVID-19," CNN, updated May 11, 2020,
    https://www.cnn.com/2020/05/11/health/hydroxychloroquine-doesnt-
    work-coronavirus/index.html.

32. Catherine Offord, "The Surgisphere Scandal: What Went Wrong?," *The
    Scientist*, October 1, 2020, https://www.the-scientist.com/features/the-
    surgisphere-scandal-what-went-wrong--67955.

33. Alex Ledsom, "France Says No to Hydroxychloroquine Prescription
    After Lancet Study," *Forbes*, May 26, 2020, https://www.forbes.

com/sites/alexledsom/2020/05/26/france-says-no-to-prescribing-hydroxychloroquine-after-lancet-study/?sh=6c7e6ea624b5.

34. Mandeep R. Mehra, Frank Ruschitzka, and Amit N. Patel, "Retraction—Hydroxychloroquine or Chloroquine With or Without a Macrolide for Treatment of COVID-19: A Multinational Registry Analysis," *The Lancet* 395, no 10240 (June 13, 2020): P1820, https://doi.org/10.1016/S0140-6736(20)31324-6.

35. Ralph Ellis, "The Lancet Retracts Hydroxychloroquine Study," WebMD, June 4, 2020, https://www.webmd.com/lung/news/20200605/lancet-retracts-hydroxychloroquine-study.

36. Mehra, Ruschitzka, and Patel, "Retraction."

37. Editors of the Lancet Group, "Learning From a Retraction," *The Lancet* 396, no. 10257 (October 10, 2020): P1056, https://doi.org/10.1016/S0140-6736(20)31958-9.

38. "Committed Grants," Bill and Melinda Gates Foundation, accessed July 2, 2021, https://www.gatesfoundation.org/about/committed-grants, download grants data file.

39. Lagier et al., "Outcomes of 3,737 COVID-19 Patients Treated With Hydroxychloroquine/Azithromycin and Other Regimens in Marseille, France"; Philippe Gautret et al., "Hydroxychloroquine and Azithromycin as a Treatment of COVID-19: Results of an Open-Label Non-Randomized Clinical Trial," *International Journal of Antimicrobial Agents* 56, no. 1 (July 2020): 105949, https://doi.org/10.1016/j.ijantimicag.2020.105949.

40. Joseph A. Ladapo, "Randomized Controlled Trials of Early Ambulatory Hydroxychloroquine in the Prevention of COVID-19 Infection, Hospitalization, and Death: Meta-Analysis," *medRxiv*, September 30, 2020, https://doi.org/10.1101/2020.09.30.20204693; Paul E. Alexander et al., "Early Multidrug Outpatient Treatment of SARS-CoV-2 Infection (COVID-19) and Reduced Mortality Among Nursing Home Residents," *medRxiv*, February 1, 2021, https://doi.org/10.1101/2021.01.28.212 50706; Harvey A. Risch, "Hydroxychloroquine in Early Treatment of High-Risk COVID-19 Outpatients: Efficacy and Safety Evidence," Trial Site News, April 8, 2021, https://trialsitenews.com/wp-content/uploads/2021/05/Evidence-Brief-Risch-v4.pdf; Harvey A. Risch, "Early Outpatient Treatment of Symptomatic, High-Risk COVID-19 Patients That Should Be Ramped Up Immediately as Key to the Pandemic Crisis," *American Journal of Epidemiology* 189, no. 11 (November 2020): 1218–1226, https://doi.org/10.1093/aje/kwaa093.

41. See, for example, Sten H. Vermund, "YSPH Statement Regarding Hydroxychloroquine," Yale School of Medicine, July 29, 2020, https://medicine.yale.edu/news-article/

ysph-statement-regarding-hydroxychloroquine/; Brian Flood, "'Don't Speak for Me': Yale Doctor Battles CNN Anchor Over Effectiveness of Hydroxychloroquine," Fox News, August 3, 2020, https://www.foxnews.com/media/risch-cnn-anchor-berman-hydroxychloroquine.

42. "Hydroxychloroquine and COVID-19," NPS Medicinewise, updated August 11, 2020, https://www.nps.org.au/hcq-and-covid-19; "New Restrictions on Prescribing Hydroxychloroquine for COVID-19," Australian Government Department of Health, March 24, 2020, https://www.tga.gov.au/alert/new-restrictions-prescribing-hydroxychloroquine-covid-19; "Amendments to the New Restrictions on Prescribing Hydroxychloroquine for COVID-19," Australian Government Department of Health, August 26, 2020, https://www.tga.gov.au/alert/amendments-new-restrictions-prescribing-hydroxychloroquine-covid-19.

43. Kimberly Wallace, "An Additional Crisis," *Trinidad Express*, updated May 11, 2020, https://webcache.googleusercontent.com/search?q=cache:sR9galzcT4gJ:https://trinidadexpress.com/features/local/an-additional-crisis/article_f18139f8-7d14-11ea-bbd4-0bc7159a5db5.html+&cd=12&hl=en&ct=clnk&gl=us.

44. Stella Immanuel, "WE NEED YOUR HELP," Facebook, July 28, 2020, 12:34 p.m., https://www.facebook.com/drstella.gwp/posts/10158800045169180.

45. "Coronavirus (COVID-19) Update: FDA Revokes Emergency Use Authorization for Chloroquine and Hydroxychloroquine," Food and Drug Administration, June 15, 2020, https://www.fda.gov/news-events/press-announcements/coronavirus-covid-19-update-fda-revokes-emergency-use-authorization-chloroquine-and.

46. Jared S. Hopkins, "States Try Reducing Malaria-Drug Hoarding Amid Unproven Coronavirus Benefit," *Wall Street Journal*, April 5, 2020, https://www.wsj.com/articles/states-try-reducing-malaria-drug-hoarding-amid-unproven-coronavirus-benefit-11586095200; "State Action on Hydroxychloroquine and Chloroquine Access," Lupus Foundation of America, accessed June 30, 2021, https://www.lupus.org/advocate/state-action-on-hydroxychloroquine-and-chloroquine-access.

47. Samia Arshad et al., "Treatment With Hydroxychloroquine, Azithromycin, and Combination in Patients Hospitalized With COVID-19," *International Journal of Infectious Diseases* 97 (August 1, 2020): 396–403, https://doi.org/10.1016/j.ijid.2020.06.099; C. Prodromos and T. Rumschlag, "Hydroxychloroquine Is Effective, and Consistently So When Provided Early, for COVID-19: A Systematic Review," *New Microbes and New Infections* 38 (November 2020): 100776, https://dx.doi.org/10.1016%2Fj.nmni.2020.100776.

48. Andrew Bazemore et al., "Proportional Erosion of the Primary Care Physician Workforce Has Continued Since 2010," *American Family Physician* 100, no. 4 (August 15, 2019): 211–212, https://www.aafp.org/afp/2019/0815/p211.html.

49. "Special Bulletin: Senate Passes the Coronavirus Aid, Relief, and Economic Security (CARES) Act," American Hospital Association, accessed July 5, 2021, https://www.aha.org/special-bulletin/2020-03-26-senate-passes-coronavirus-aid-relief-and-economic-security-cares-act; Michelle Rogers, "Fact Check: Hospitals Get Paid More if Patients Listed as COVID-19, on Ventilators," *USA Today*, updated April 27, 2020, https://www.usatoday.com/story/news/factcheck/2020/04/24/fact-check-medicare-hospitals-paid-more-covid-19-patients-coronavirus/3000638001/.

50. Neena Satija, "'I Do Regret Being There': Simone Gold, Noted Hydroxychloroquine Advocate, Was Inside the Capitol During the Riot," *Washington Post*, January 12, 2021, https://www.washingtonpost.com/investigations/simone-gold-capitol-riot-coronavirus/2021/01/12/d1d39e84-545f-11eb-a817-e5e7f8a406d6_story.html.

CHAPTER 6

1. Wayne J. Guglielmo, "Doc Who Used Hydroxychloroquine Met Standard of Care, Says Med Board; More," Medscape, November 3, 2020, https://www.medscape.com/viewarticle/940264.

2. Ben Billups, "Video: Dr. Robin Armstrong Explains Use of Hydroxychloroquine to Treat Coronavirus," *The Texan*, April 22, 2020, https://thetexan.news/hydroxychloroquine-coronavirus-treatment-robin-armstrong-video-podcast/; John Wayne Ferguson, "11 County Deaths Connected to Resort at Texas City," *Galveston Daily News*, May 14, 2020, https://www.galvnews.com/news/free/article_c0084ebc-b879-55fa-9eca-1b2f8ba98ee2.html.

3. "Robin Lynn Armstrong," Texas Medical Board, June 30, 2021, https://profile.tmb.state.tx.us/BoardActions.aspx?9190dafd-f0db-45f4-bc8c-59b3248cfc38.

4. Randy Wallace, "Fox 26 Gets Unprecedented Access to Texas' 1st Nursing Home to Treat COVID-19 With Hydroxychloroquine," Fox 26, April 27, 2020, https://www.fox26houston.com/news/fox-26-gets-unprecedented-access-to-texas-1st-nursing-home-to-treat-covid-19-with-hydroxychloroquine.

5. Arturo Garcia, "Is a Texas Doctor Curing COVID-19 Patients For $50?," Truth or Fiction, July 10, 2020, https://www.truthorfiction.com/my-name-is-brian-c-procter-covid-19/.

6. Henrique Pott-Junior et al., "Use of Ivermectin in the Treatment of COVID-19: A Pilot Trial," *Toxicology Reports* 8 (2021): 505–510, https://doi.org/10.1016/j.toxrep.2021.03.003; Dhyuti Gupta et al., "Ivermectin: Potential Candidate for the Treatment of COVID 19," *Brazilian Journal of Infectious Diseases* 24, no. 4 (July–August 2020), https://doi.org/10.1016/j.bjid.2020.06.002; Fabio Rocha Formiga, "Ivermectin: An Award-Winning Drug With Expected Antiviral Activity Against COVID-19," *Journal of Controlled Release* 329, no. 10 (January 2021): 758–761, https://doi.org/10.1016/j.jconrel.2020.10.009.

7. Bob Hall, "Media Interview With 'Boots-on-the-Ground' Doctors and Professionals Actively Treating COVID With Early Intervention Treatment," Facebook, August 12, 2020, https://www.facebook.com/333132016713859/videos/1639776369536397.

8. Bob Hall, "ICYM my two page letter," Facebook, August 18, 2020, https://www.facebook.com/SenatorBobHall/photos/p.3838440946182931/3838440946182931?type=3.

9. "First Case of Corona Virus Disease Confirmed in Nigeria," Nigeria Centre for Disease Control, February 28, 2020, https://ncdc.gov.ng/news/227/first-case-of-corona-virus-disease-confirmed-in-nigeria.

10. Xinhua, "Malaria in Decline; End Seen by 2020," State Council of the People's Republic of China, updated April 25, 2018, http://english.www.gov.cn/news/top_news/2018/04/25/content_281476123471576.htm.

11. "Melinda Gates: COVID-19 Will Be Horrible in the Developing World," CNN, April 10, 2020, https://www.cnn.com/videos/business/2020/04/10/melinda-gates-coronavirus.cnn-business.

12. "Nigeria," World Health Organization, accessed July 3, 2021, https://covid19.who.int/region/afro/country/ng; "United States of America," World Health Organization, accessed July 3, 2021, https://covid19.who.int/region/amro/country/us.

13. "COVID-19 (WHO African Region)," World Health Organization, accessed July 3, 2021, https://who.maps.arcgis.com/apps/dashboards/0c9b3a8b68d0437a8cf28581e9c063a9.

14. "Malaria Introduction," National Department of Health, Republic of South Africa, accessed July 3, 2021, http://www.health.gov.za/malaria/.

15. Kai Kupferschmidt, "First-of-Its-Kind African Trial Tests Common Drugs to Prevent Severe COVID-19," *Science*, December 3, 2020, https://www.sciencemag.org/news/2020/12/first-its-kind-african-trial-tests-common-drugs-prevent-severe-covid-19+&cd=12&hl=en&ct=clnk&gl=us; Kerry Cullinan, "Regulators Under Pressure as Illegal Use of Ivermectin to Treat COVID-19 Soars," Health Policy Watch, May 2, 2021, https://healthpolicy-watch.news/regulators-under-pressure-as-illegal-use-of-ivermectin-to-treat-covid-19-soars/;

Daryl Nzokou Tcheutchoua et al., "Unexpected Low Burden of Coronavirus Disease 2019 (COVID-19) in Sub-Saharan Africa Region Despite Disastrous Predictions: Reasons and Perspectives," *Pan African Medical Journal* 37 (December 16, 2020): 352, https://doi.org/10.11604/pamj.2020.37.352.25254; Hisaya Tanioka, "Why COVID-19 Is Not So Spread in Africa: How Does Ivermectin Affect It?," *medRxiv*, March 26, 2021, https://doi.org/10.1101/2021.03.26.21254377.

16. Pierre Kory et al., "Review of the Emerging Evidence Demonstrating the Efficacy of Ivermectin in the Prophylaxis and Treatment of COVID-19," *American Journal of Therapeutics* 28, no. 3 (May–June 2021): e299–e318, https://www.ncbi.nlm.nih.gov/pmc/articles/PMC8088823/.

17. "India," World Health Organization, accessed July 3, 2021, https://covid19.who.int/region/searo/country/in.

18. See, for example, "Pakistan," World Health Organization, accessed July 3, 2021, https://covid19.who.int/region/emro/country/pk; "Venezuela (Bolivarian Republic of)," Health Organization, accessed July 3, 2021, https://covid19.who.int/region/amro/country/ve.

19. "HCQ for COVID-19," COVID-19 Early Treatment, accessed July 6, 2021, https://c19hcq.com/.

20. "Senate Hearing on COVID-19 Outpatient Treatment," C-Span, November 19, 2020, https://www.c-span.org/video/?478159-1/senate-hearing-covid-19-outpatient-treatment.

21. Kelvin Chan and Barbara Ortutay, "Facebook Panel Overturns 4 Content Takedowns in First Ruling," Associated Press, January 28, 2021, https://apnews.com/article/facebook-oversight-board-ruling-c6f6b20a4a6d5a208cebaa143412d3e5.

Chapter 7

1. Bob Hall, "Happening NOW! (NOTE: Dr. Richard P. Bartlett, M.D. has an unforeseen conflict the first part of this hour. Be sure to view through the full LIVE video to not miss his great feedback as he joins in!)," Facebook, July 15, 2020, 8:00 p.m., https://www.facebook.com/333132016713859/videos/305111243951303.

2. "Goya Foods CEO Bob Unanue Refuses to Bow to Leftist Cancel Culture Mob," Fox News, July 10, 2020, https://www.foxnews.com/transcript/goya-foods-ceo-bob-unanue-refuses-to-bow-to-leftist-cancel-culture-mob.

3. "We Have Been Lied To—American Doctors Address COVID-19 Misinformation at SCOTUS Press Conference," BitChute, July 28, 2020, https://www.bitchute.com/video/zr04GsUupOwk/.

4. Travis M. Andrews and Danielle Paquette, "Trump Retweeted a Video With False COVID-19 Claims. One Doctor in It Has Said Demons Cause

Illnesses," *Washington Post*, July 29, 2020, https://www.washingtonpost.
com/technology/2020/07/28/stella-immanuel-hydroxychloroquine-video-
trump-americas-frontline-doctors/.

5. Andrews and Paquette, "Trump Retweeted a Video With False
   COVID-19 Claims."

6. Rachel Lerman, Katie Shepherd, and Taylor Telford, "Twitter Penalizes
   Donald Trump Jr. for Posting Hydroxychloroquine Misinformation
   Amid Coronavirus Pandemic," *Washington Post*, July 28, 2020, https://
   www.washingtonpost.com/nation/2020/07/28/trump-coronavirus-
   misinformation-twitter/.

7. Travis M. Andrews, "Madonna Keeps Making Controversial COVID-19
   Claims, Calling a Misinformation-Spreading Doctor Her 'Hero,'"
   Washington Post, July 29, 2020, https://www.washingtonpost.com/
   technology/2020/07/29/madonna-instagram-covid-coronavirus-stella-
   immanuel-bathtub/.

8. CNN, "CNN's Dr. Sanjay Gupta uncovers his roots," YouTube, October
   20, 2014, https://www.youtube.com/watch?v=d9ivklq8q7U.

9. Tom Foreman, "Exorcist Casting the Devil Out of Tulsa," Anderson
   Cooper 360 (blog), March 26, 2006, http://www.cnn.com/CNN/
   Programs/anderson.cooper.360/blog/2006/03/exorcist-casting-devil-out-
   of-tulsa.html.

10. Adam Edelman, "Biden Slams Trump for Promoting False COVID-19
    Claims From 'Crazy Woman,'" NBC News, July 29, 2020, https://www.
    nbcnews.com/politics/2020-election/biden-slams-trump-promoting-
    false-covid-19-claims-crazy-woman-n1235235.

11. Will Sommer, "Trump's New Favorite COVID Doctor Believes in
    Alien DNA, Demon Sperm, and Hydroxychloroquine," *Daily Beast*,
    updated July 28, 2020, https://www.thedailybeast.com/stella-immanuel-
    trumps-new-covid-doctor-believes-in-alien-dna-demon-sperm-
    and-hydroxychloroquine; Brandon W. Hawk, "The Ancient Lore of
    Demons, Sex, and Sickness," *Daily Beast*, August 1, 2020, https://www.
    thedailybeast.com/dr-stella-immanuels-beliefs-are-rooted-in-ancient-
    lore-of-demons-sex-and-sickness.

12. "Trump Promoted a Doctor. Watch What She Said About Demons,"
    CNN, July 29, 2020, https://edition.cnn.com/videos/politics/2020/07/29/
    donald-trump-coronavirus-doctor-kth-sot-vpx-ac360.cnn.

13. Veronica Stracqualursi, "Trump Promotes a Doctor Who Has Claimed
    Alien DNA Was Used in Medical Treatments," CNN, July 29, 2020,
    https://www.cnn.com/2020/07/29/politics/stella-immanuel-trump-
    doctor/index.html.

14. Stracqualursi, "Trump Promotes a Doctor Who Has Claimed Alien
    DNA Was Used in Medical Treatments."

15. Sarah Al-Arshani, "Rudy Giuliani Interviewed Dr. Stella Immanuel—Doctor Who Previously Preached About Alien DNA—on His Radio Show Calling Her His 'Hero,'" *Business Insider*, July 30, 2020, https://www.businessinsider.com/rudy-giuliani-stella-immanuel-demon-sperm-radio-hero-2020-7.

16. Charisma News Staff, "COVID-Busting Warrior Physician Stella Immanuel: 'America, You Don't Need to Be Afraid,'" *Charisma*, August 2, 2020, https://www.charismamag.com/life/culture/46110-covid-busting-warrior-physician-stella-immanuel-america-you-don-t-need-to-be-afraid.

17. "Alex Jones (3rd Hour)," BitChute, May 19, 2021, https://www.bitchute.com/video/eoRST1Tgd4lU/.

18. Stella Immanuel, "This is my reply to someone, a fellow physician on another social media platform, that was going on and on about me appearing on Alex Jones," Telemetrio, May 21, 2021, 2:52 a.m., https://telemetr.io/en/channels/1467327751-realdrstella/posts.

19. KPRC2 / Click2Houston, "'We see patients day one and put them on hydroxychloroquine [and by] day ten, they test negative. It is a cure. I don't know why people are getting crazy about this,' Dr. Stella Immanuel said," Facebook, July 31, 2020, 6:00 a.m., https://www.facebook.com/permalink.php?id=110260895670639&story_fbid=3789774501052575.

20. PragerU, "The Candace Owens Show: Dr. Stella Immanuel," YouTube, November 15, 2020, https://www.youtube.com/watch?v=5g7EWA9GFkQ.

CHAPTER 8

1. James Lawler, "You Asked, We Answered: Do the COVID-19 Vaccines Contain Aborted Fetal Cells?," Nebraska Medicine, March 2, 2021, https://www.nebraskamed.com/COVID/you-asked-we-answered-do-the-covid-19-vaccines-contain-aborted-fetal-cells.

2. Miriam Fauzia, "Fact Check: Israel Launching 'Green Pass' for Citizens Vaccinated Against COVID-19," *USA Today*, updated March 3, 2021, https://www.usatoday.com/story/news/factcheck/2021/03/02/fact-check-israel-launching-green-pass-covid-19-vaccinated/6871965002/; "What Is a Green Pass?," Israel Ministry of Health, accessed July 7, 2021, https://corona.health.gov.il/en/directives/green-pass-info/.

3. One America News Network, "Houston Doctor Successfully Treated Over 20K Patients With Hydroxychloroquine," Rumble, April 16, 2021, https://rumble.com/vfqkcp-houston-doctor-successfully-treated-over-20k-patients-with-hydroxychloroqui.html.

4. One America News Network, "Houston Doctor Successfully Treated Over 20K Patients With Hydroxychloroquine."

5. One America News Network, "Houston Doctor Successfully Treated Over 20K Patients With Hydroxychloroquine."

6. Husch Blackwell, "50 State Update on Pending Legislation Pertaining to Employer-Mandated Vaccinations," JD Supra, March 5, 2021, https://www.jdsupra.com/legalnews/50-state-update-on-pending-legislation-3726932/.

7. See, for example, "Myocarditis and Pericarditis Following mRNA COVID-19 Vaccination," Centers for Disease Control and Prevention, June 23, 2021, https://www.cdc.gov/coronavirus/2019-ncov/vaccines/safety/myocarditis.html.

8. Nikolaj Skydsgaard and Jacob Gronholt-pedersen, "In World First, Denmark Ditches AstraZeneca's COVID-19 Shot," Reuters, April 14, 2021, https://www.reuters.com/world/europe/world-first-denmark-ditches-astrazenecas-covid-19-shot-2021-04-14/.

9. "Joint CDC and FDA Statement on Johnson & Johnson COVID-19 Vaccine," Centers for Disease Control and Prevention, April 13, 2021, https://www.cdc.gov/media/releases/2021/s0413-JJ-vaccine.html.

CHAPTER 9

1. "Fwd: Dinner," WikiLeaks, accessed July 12, 2021, https://wikileaks.org/podesta-emails/emailid/15893.

2. Parag Verma et al., "A Statistical Analysis of Impact of COVID19 on the Global Economy and Stock Index Returns," *SN Computer Science* 2, no. 27 (2021), https://doi.org/10.1007/s42979-020-00410-w.

3. "ILO Monitor: COVID-19 and the World of Work. Seventh edition," International Labour Organization, January 25, 2021, https://www.ilo.org/wcmsp5/groups/public/@dgreports/@dcomm/documents/briefingnote/wcms_767028.pdf.

4. Larry Elliott, "IMF Estimates Global COVID Cost at $28tn in Lost Output," *The Guardian*, October 13, 2020, https://www.theguardian.com/business/2020/oct/13/imf-covid-cost-world-economic-outlook.

5. Lora Jones, Daniele Palumbo & David Brown, "Coronavirus: How the Pandemic Has Changed the World Economy," BBC, January 24, 2021, https://www.bbc.com/news/business-51706225.

6. Realdrstella, "COVID19 Treatment and Prevention Protocol in Layman's Terms From Dr. Stella Immanuel MD to Africa," Rumble, January 18, 2021, https://rumble.com/vcyr0z-covid19-treatment-and-prevention-protocol-in-laymans-terms-from-dr.-stella-.html.

7. Mohammad Tariqur Rahman and Syed Zahir Idid, "Can Zn Be a Critical Element in COVID-19 Treatment?," *Biological Trace Element Research* (May 26, 2020): 1-9, https://dx.doi.org/10.1007%2Fs12011-020-02194-9.
8. "COVID19 Supplements (covidvites)," Frontline MDs with Dr. Stella Immanuel, accessed July 12, 2021, https://frontlinemds.com/covid19-supplements-covidvites/.
9. "Carrying the Mantle—Sharing the Legacy of Maria Woodworth Etter," Lite the Fire, accessed July 7, 2021, https://www.litethefire.org/maria_woodworth_etter.
10. J. Lee Grady, "How I Stir My Faith During Troubled Times," Faith New Network, accessed July 7, 2021, https://www.faithnews.cc/?p=30412.

CHAPTER 10

1. D. M. Woodbury et al., "Effects of Carbon Dioxide on Brain Excitability and Electrolytes," *American Journal of Physiology* 192, no. 1 (January 1958): 79–90, https://doi.org/10.1152/ajplegacy.1957.192.1.79.
2. M. Kiray et al., "Effects of Carbon Dioxide Exposure on Early Brain Development in Rats," *Biotechnic and Histochemistry* 89, no. 5 (July 2014): 371–383, https://doi.org/10.3109/10520295.2013.872298.
3. Feng Xu et al., "The Influence of Carbon Dioxide on Brain Activity and Metabolism in Conscious Humans," *Journal of Cerebral Blood Flow and Metabolism* 31, no. 1 (January 2011): 58–67, https://dx.doi.org/10.1038%2Fjcbfm.2010.153.

CHAPTER 11

1. Wei Qi, Martin Gevonden, and Arieh Shalev, "Prevention of Post-Traumatic Stress Disorder After Trauma: Current Evidence and Future Directions," *Current Psychiatry Reports* 18, no. 20 (2016), https://dx.doi.org/10.1007%2Fs11920-015-0655-0.
2. L. Stoppelbein, L. Greening, and Paula Fitec, "The Role of Cortisol in PTSD Among Women Exposed to a Trauma-Related Stressor," *Journal of Anxiety Disorders* 26, no. 2 (March 2012): 352–358, https://dx.doi.org/10.1016%2Fj.janxdis.2011.12.004.
3. Inger Agger et al., "Testimonial Therapy. A Pilot Project to Improve Psychological Wellbeing Among Survivors of Torture in India," *Torture: Quarterly Journal on Rehabilitation of Torture Victims and Prevention of Torture* 19, no. 3 (January 2009): 204–217, https://www.researchgate.net/publication/40908122_Testimonial_therapy_A_pilot_project_to_improve_psychological_wellbeing_among_survivors_of_torture_in_India.

4. Gina Forster et al., "The Role of the Amygdala in Anxiety Disorders," *The Amygdala—A Discrete Multitasking Manager* (December 19, 2012), https://doi.org/10.5772/50323.

5. "The Holmes-Rahe Life Stress Inventory," Stress.org, accessed July 13, 2021, https://www.stress.org/wp-content/uploads/2019/04/stress-inventory-1.pdf.

6. M. Harvey Brenner, "Commentary: Economic Growth Is the Basis of Mortality Rate Decline in the 20th Century—Experience of the United States 1901–2000," *International Journal of Epidemiology* 34, no. 6 (December 2005): 1214–1221, https://doi.org/10.1093/ije/dyi146.

7. Maxime Taquet et al., "Bidirectional Associations Between COVID-19 and Psychiatric Disorder: Retrospective Cohort Studies of 62 354 COVID-19 Cases in the USA," *The Lancet Psychiatry* 8, no. 2 (February 1, 2021): 130–140, https://doi.org/10.1016/S2215-0366(20)30462-4; Nirmita Panchal et al., "The Implications of COVID-19 for Mental Health and Substance Use," KFF, February 10, 2021, https://www.kff.org/coronavirus-covid-19/issue-brief/the-implications-of-covid-19-for-mental-health-and-substance-use/; Mark É. Czeisler et al., "Mental Health, Substance Use, and Suicidal Ideation During the COVID-19 Pandemic—United States, June 24–30, 2020," *Morbidity and Mortality Weekly Report* 69, no. 32 (August 14, 2020): 1049–1057, https://www.cdc.gov/mmwr/volumes/69/wr/mm6932a1.htm; Francesca Solmi, James L. Downs, and Dasha E. Nicholls, "COVID-19 and Eating Disorders in Young People," *The Lancet Child & Adolescent Health* 5, no. 5 (May 1, 2021): 316–318, https://doi.org/10.1016/S2352-4642(21)00094-8; "The Impact of COVID-19 on Pediatric Mental Health," *FAIR Health*, March 2, 2021, https://s3.amazonaws.com/media2.fairhealth.org/whitepaper/asset/The%20Impact%20of%20COVID-19%20on%20Pediatric%20Mental%20Health%20-%20A%20Study%20of%20Private%20Healthcare%20Claims%20-%20A%20FAIR%20Health%20White%20Paper.pdf; Kim Usher et al., "Family Violence and COVID⊠19: Increased Vulnerability and Reduced Options for Support," *International Journal of Mental Health Nursing* 7 (May 2020), https://dx.doi.org/10.1111%2Finm.12735.

8. Monica Malowney, Sarah Keltz Daniel Fischer, and J. Wesley Boyd, "Availability of Outpatient Care From Psychiatrists: A Simulated-Patient Study in Three U.S. Cities," *Psychiatric Services*, January 2, 2015, https://doi.org/10.1176/appi.ps.201400051.

9. Olga Khazan, "Psychiatric Patients Wait in ERs for Days and Weeks as Inpatient Beds Are Scaled Back," *Washington Post*, January 22, 2013, https://www.washingtonpost.com/local/psychiatric-patients-wait-in-ers-as-inpatient-beds-are-scaled-back/2013/01/22/28c61b5e-56b7-11e2-a613-ec8d394535c6_story.html.

10. Jason G. Goldman, "Ed Tronick and the 'Still Face Experiment,'" *Scientific American*, October 18, 2010, https://blogs.scientificamerican. com/thoughtful-animal/ed-tronick-and-the-8220-still-face-experiment-8221/.

11. M. Katherine Weinberg et al., "Effects of Maternal Depression and Panic Disorder on Mother–Infant Interactive Behavior in the Face-to-Face Still-Face Paradigm," *Infant Mental Health Journal* 29, no. 5 (September–October 2008): 472–491, https://dx.doi. org/10.1002%2Fimhj.20193.

12. Mélissa C. Allé and Dorthe Berntsen, "Self-Isolation, Psychotic Symptoms, and Cognitive Problems During the COVID-19 Worldwide Outbreak," *Psychiatry Research* 302 (August 2021): 114015, https:// dx.doi.org/10.1016%2Fj.psychres.2021.114015.

13. Sarah LeTrent, "When a Friend Won't Walk Away From Abuse," CNN, updated January 10, 2013, https://www.cnn.com/2013/01/10/living/ friend-domestic-abuse.

14. Sayamwong E. Hammack, Matthew A. Cooper, and Kimberly R. Lezak, "Overlapping Neurobiology of Learned Helplessness and Conditioned Defeat: Implications for PTSD and Mood Disorders," *Neuropharmacology* 62, no. 2 (February 2012): 565–575, https://dx.doi. org/10.1016%2Fj.neuropharm.2011.02.024.

15. "Interim Public Health Recommendations for Fully Vaccinated People," Centers for Disease Control and Prevention, May 28, 2021, https://www. cdc.gov/coronavirus/2019-ncov/vaccines/fully-vaccinated-guidance. html.

16. Wikipedia, s.v. "Learned helplessness," last edited June 14, 2021, https:// en.wikipedia.org/wiki/Learned_helplessness.

17. Martin E. P. Seligman, "Learned Helplessness," *Annual Review of Medicine* 23 (February 1972): 407–412, https://doi.org/10.1146/annurev. me.23.020172.002203.

CHAPTER 12

1. "Pneumonia of Unknown Cause—China," World Health Organization, January 5, 2020, https://web.archive.org/web/20200107032945/https:// www.who.int/csr/don/05-january-2020-pneumonia-of-unkown-cause-china/en/.

2. "LAX Passenger Quarantined After Showing Potential Coronavirus Symptoms," Fox 5 New York, January 23, 2020, https://www.fox5ny.com/ news/lax-passenger-quarantined-after-showing-potential-coronavirus-symptoms.

3. "Coronavirus Disease 2019 in Children—United States, February 12–April 2, 2020," *Morbidity and Mortality Weekly Report* 69, no. 14 (April 10, 2020): 422–426, http://dx.doi.org/10.15585/mmwr.mm6914e4.

4. Ping-Ing Lee et al., "Are Children Less Susceptible to COVID-19?," *Journal of Microbiology, Immunology and Infection* 53, no. 3 (June 2020): 371–372, https://dx.doi.org/10.1016%2Fj.jmii.2020.02.011;

5. Alain Fischer, "Resistance of Children to COVID-19. How?," *Mucosal Immunology* 13 (2020): 563–565, https://doi.org/10.1038/s41385-020-0303-9.

6. Daniel Horn, "The Pandemic Could Put Your Doctor Out of Business," *Washington Post*, April 24, 2020, https://www.washingtonpost.com/outlook/2020/04/24/pandemic-could-put-your-doctor-out-business/.

7. A Brighter Tomorrow Pediatrics, "Worried about Coronavirus???," Facebook, February 26, 2020, 2:00 p.m., https://www.facebook.com/101847483241104/videos/245667386442644.

8. Mike Stobbe, "APNewsBreak: 80,000 People Died of Flu Last Winter in US," Associated Press, September 26, 2018, https://apnews.com/article/health-north-america-centers-for-disease-control-and-prevention-ap-top-news-us-news-818b5360eb7d472480ebde13da5c72b5.

9. "Overview of TMC ICU Bed Capacity and Occupancy," Texas Medical Center, archived June 29, 2020, https://web.archive.org/web/20200629145323/https://www.tmc.edu/coronavirus-updates/overview-of-tmc-icu-bed-capacity-and-occupancy/; "Overview of TMC ICU Bed Capacity and Occupancy," Texas Medical Center, archived September 16, 2020, https://web.archive.org/web/20200916172159/https://www.tmc.edu/coronavirus-updates/overview-of-tmc-icu-bed-capacity-and-occupancy/.

10. A Brighter Tomorrow Pediatrics, "Doc in the Box #27: Just the numbers...," Facebook, June 26, 2020, 6:44 p.m., https://www.facebook.com/101847483241104/videos/632244874302438; A Brighter Tomorrow Pediatrics, "Doc in the Box #31: Just the numbers Part 2...I'm back!," Facebook, September 1, 2020, 7:19 p.m., https://www.facebook.com/101847483241104/videos/1040664173032237.

11. A Brighter Tomorrow Pediatrics, "Doc in the Box #29: Should kids go to school?," Facebook, July 8, 2020, 68:19 p.m., https://www.facebook.com/101847483241104/videos/711548972749496.

12. "SARS-CoV-2–Associated Deaths Among Persons Aged <21 Years—United States, February 12–July 31, 2020," *Morbidity and Mortality Weekly Report* 69, no. 37 (September 18, 2020): 1324–1329, http://dx.doi.org/10.15585/mmwr.mm6937e4.

13. Yuanyuan Dong et al., "Epidemiology of COVID-19 Among Children in China," *Pediatrics* 145, no. 6 (June 2020): e20200702, https://doi.org/10.1542/peds.2020-0702.

14. Peter A. McCullough et al., "Pathophysiological Basis and Rationale for Early Outpatient Treatment of SARS-CoV-2 (COVID-19) Infection," *American Journal of Medicine* 134, no. 1 (January 2021): 16–22, https://dx.doi.org/10.1016%2Fj.amjmed.2020.07.003.

15. Peter Wade, "Doctor Used Republican Connections to Get Unproven, Trump-Endorsed Meds to Treat Unknowing Elderly COVID-19 Patients," *Rolling Stone*, April 11, 2020, https://www.rollingstone.com/politics/politics-news/republican-doctor-trump-unproven-medicine-elderly-coronavirus-patients-982337/.

16. Marine1063, "Uncensored Truth Tour—Stafford TX—MAY 16, 2021," BitChute, May 18, 2021, https://www.bitchute.com/video/rcPJgpFlIiYw/.

17. Leah Croll, "Why AstraZeneca Pausing Its COVID-19 Vaccine Trial May Be Good News," ABC News, September 9, 2020, https://abcnews.go.com/Health/astrazeneca-pausing-covid-19-vaccine-trial-good-news/story?id=72903384; "Johnson & Johnson Prepares to Resume Phase 3 ENSEMBLE Trial of Its Janssen COVID-19 Vaccine Candidate in the U.S.," Johnson & Johnson, updated October 23, 2020, https://www.jnj.com/our-company/johnson-johnson-prepares-to-resume-phase-3-ensemble-trial-of-its-janssen-covid-19-vaccine-candidate-in-the-us.

18. "Suspension of Rotavirus Vaccine After Reports of Intussusception—United States, 1999," *Morbidity and Mortality Weekly Report* 53, no. 34 (September 3, 2004): 786–789, https://www.cdc.gov/mmwr/preview/mmwrhtml/mm5334a3.htm.

19. Shari Roan, "Swine Flu 'Debacle' of 1976 Is Recalled," *Los Angeles Times*, April 27, 2009, https://www.latimes.com/archives/la-xpm-2009-apr-27-sci-swine-history27-story.html.

20. "The Vaccine Adverse Event Reporting System (VAERS) Results," Centers for Disease Control and Prevention, accessed July 14, 2021, https://wonder.cdc.gov/controller/datarequest/D8;jsessionid=64E15120 71F1B37BF8C484ACF08A?stage=results&action=sort&direction=MEA SURE_DESCEND&measure=D8.M1.

Chapter 13

1. Mary Ann Levy, *The Luciferian Strategy* (Port Harcourt, Nigeria: Spiritual Life Outreach, 2018). Used with permission.

2. George Orwell, *1984* (Thorndike, ME: G. K. Hall, 2001), 52, https://archive.org/details/1984novel00orwe_0/page/52/mode/2up?q=controls.

CHAPTER 15

1. A ten-point plan to destroy Christianity is widely attributed to Alice
   Bailey, whom some consider a founder of the modern new age movement,
   but her authorship could not be confirmed, and the original source of
   the ten-point plan could not be identified. See, for instance, Stewart
   Kabatebate, "Alice Bailey 10 Point Plan to Destroy Christianity," Inspired
   Walk, accessed August 17, 2021, https://www.inspiredwalk.com/6297/
   alice-baileys-10-point-plan-to-destroy-christianity and "Alice Bailey's
   10-Point Plan for the Destruction of Christianity," accessed August
   17, 2021, https://files.secure.website/wscfus/10348600/28415701/alice-
   baileys-10-point-plan-to-destroy-christianity.pdf.